CW00545008

The Chrysanthemum Throne

This book is dedicated to the memory
of my beloved granddaughter
Natasha Helen Martin (1992–1996)

THE CHRYSANTHEMUM THRONE

A History of the Emperors of Japan

PETER MARTIN

SUTTON PUBLISHING

First published in the United Kingdom in 1997 by
Sutton Publishing Limited · Phoenix Mill
Thrupp · Stroud · Gloucestershire · GL5 2BU

British Library Cataloguing in Publication Data
A catalogue record for this book is available from the British Library.

ISBN 0-7509-1203-0

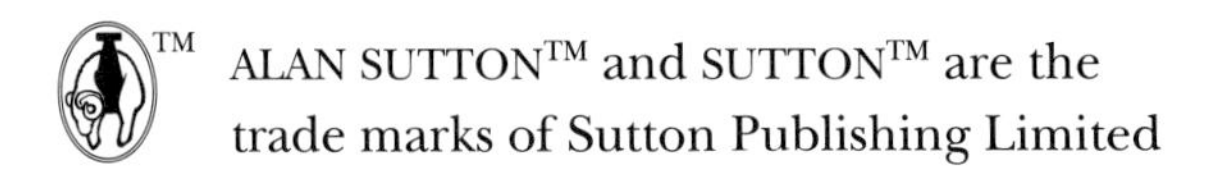

Typeset in 10/15.5 pt New Baskerville.
Typesetting and origination by
Sutton Publishing Limited.
Printed in Great Britain by
Butler & Tanner, Frome, Somerset.

Contents

List of Colour Plates

Acknowledgements

My aims and objectives in writing this book were modest, for I am an amateur historian, and make no claim to scholarly originality. My interest in the history of the Japanese throne is due in great measure to the fact that I lived in Japan in privileged circumstances for a total of eleven years, and by good fortune was able to meet a number of people who moved in and, in the case of some, were born into imperial circles.

I was first sent to Japan in 1963 by the British Council, to oversee its work in Kyoto and the surrounding Kansai region, in a state of almost perfect ignorance of Japanese history and culture. Unlike new members of the British diplomatic service assigned to Japan, I did not receive full-time language training, nor was I given much in the way of background briefing. So I was obliged to grapple with the language and try to learn about a new and in many ways alien culture in my spare time. I greatly enjoyed fending for myself, buoyed by the generous advice of the many Japanese and expatriate acquaintances of a variety of nationalities whom I soon made.

After a month or two it began to sink in that I was living in the historic heartland of Japan, in a city which had been the imperial capital for a thousand years. Quite often I wondered if it was all a dream, or whether I really was being paid to live five minutes' walk away from the temple of the Silver Pavilion, and within a short tramcar ride of the old imperial palace and countless historic shrines, temples and their gardens.

In those more spacious days it was part of my job to cosset and escort many visiting British VIPs, whose programmes inevitably included a day or two off for sightseeing in Kyoto and nearby Nara; and in that connection one of the first senior Japanese officials I had dealings with was the head of the Kyoto office of the Imperial Household Agency. For most Japanese, to obtain an agency permit to visit the imperial villas at Katsura and Shugakuin is an impossible dream, or at best a once-in-a-lifetime privilege;

yet in my capacity as escort of great and good visitors I went to both places more times than I can remember, and was given rare access to many other buildings and collections which are not normally open to the public. These experiences for me constituted a unique cram course in Japanese cultural history, and attended the birth of an interest in Japanese studies which has absorbed me ever since.

There were very few long-term resident westerners in Kyoto in the sixties, but the British Council library provided a haven for a stream of visiting American and European students and scholars, who stayed for a few days, weeks or months, and who furthered my informal education in things Japanese. Among them were graduate researchers, many of whom have since achieved eminence in the field of Japanese studies, as well as such senior authorities as Carmen Blacker, Geoffrey Bownas and the late Ivan Morris. I gratefully acknowledge the debts I owe to those named, who fuelled my growing amateur enthusiasm in the sixties. There were many others. The bilingual Otis and Alice Cary lived at Amherst House on the Doshisha University campus, and were generous friends and patient instructors (and Dr Cary in her professional capacity may well have saved my life). My closest and dearest friends were my American opposite number Mark Peattie and Alice his wife, and through them I met another United States Information Service officer, Tom Rimer, who was working in Kobe; he and Mark Peattie both later became eminent Japanese studies specialists and professors. So did Joseph Moran, another friend who was then lecturer in English at Hiroshima University and went on to become Professor of Japanese at Stirling University.

I left Kyoto in 1970, but returned to Japan in 1979, having been assigned to Tokyo. There I met other distinguished western scholars such as Edward Seidensticker, Donald Keene and Arthur Stockwin, and my work brought me into contact with a great many Japanese authorities on every conceivable subject, including history. Whether they knew it or not, these and many others taught me a great deal for which I shall always be grateful.

Throughout my seven years in Kyoto and four in Tokyo a decade later I attended a host of official functions and was presented to many members of the imperial family. With some of these I had the opportunity to enjoy private conversations; most notably with the present emperor when he was crown prince, with the present empress, and with their children. The late Princess Chichibu was the active patron of the Japan-British Society of Tokyo when I served on its council from 1979 till 1983. Knowing and talking to her, and to other Anglophiles who had been at the very centre of the turmoil of Japanese history in the past fifty years, was a rare pleasure and privilege. I particularly cherish the memory of Kazuko Aso DBE, who as a girl in February 1936 played a heroic role in defence of her grandfather Count Makino against his would-be assassins in the abortive army coup d'état. Nor shall I ever forget the late Yoshihiro Tokugawa, prominent member of the family which gave its name to a period of over two hundred years of Japanese history.

In the writing of this book I was given much encouragement and unstinting practical help by a number of friends, including Mark Peattie whose name I have already mentioned and who also read an early version of my manuscript. His comments have led to major changes, I hope for the better. From Japan I was provided with invaluable material by Shigeyuki Hirata, a friend for well over thirty years, and by Mark Schreiber, whose unique expertise and multiplicity of contacts in high and low places never cease to astound me. In Britain I am indebted to Victor Harris of the British Museum's Department of Japanese Antiquities and to his colleagues Sally Morton, Dylan Jackson and Floyd Beckford. I thank Stephen McEnally of the Japan Foundation for his good advice, and Phillip Judge for greatly enhancing the appearance of the book. He prepared the maps and plans, and reproduced the imperial crest and the impression of the imperial seal.

Carole Rawcliffe cast an historian's eye over everything I have written, pointed out where I was floundering in perilous waters, and made me more careful. She is, however, in no way to be held responsible for anything in this book, except that she improved my syntax, and most generously compiled the index.

Introduction

> The emperor shall be the symbol of the State and of the unity of the people, deriving his position from the will of the people in whom resides sovereign power.
>
> (The Japanese Constitution of 1947, Article 1)

A curious problem faces anyone who attempts in the closing years of the twentieth century to write a history of the Japanese monarchy. It arises from the fact that, until fifty years ago, the approved official Japanese account of the origins of the empire and of its earliest sovereigns before about the fifth century AD was wildly at variance with what every independent expert held to be the historical evidence. Among the dramatic consequences of defeat in the Second World War in 1945 was the immediate abandonment of the distinctive ideology upon which the government of Japan had been based for nearly a century and which had been rigidly upheld throughout the conflict. Having theoretically wielded supreme power and, like his father and grandfather before him, had the status of a living god, in 1946 the then emperor renounced any claim to divinity. The terms of the new Japanese constitution which came into effect in the following year provided for the retention of the hereditary monarchy, but underlined the purely token status of the occupant of the throne.

So the legendary first emperor Jimmu has, for all but a few elderly diehards, come to occupy a place in the Japanese national consciousness not unlike that which King Arthur has for the English. However, within living memory every Japanese schoolchild was taught that Jimmu was not only a real person, but that he assumed formal sovereignty over the Japanese nation on the eleventh day of February in the year 660 BC, at Kashihara in the province of Yamato, not far from Nara. The 2,600th anniversary of this specific date was solemnly celebrated, on 26 February 1940, in the presence of the man acclaimed as Japan's one hundred and twenty-fourth emperor and members of his family, government ministers, high officials and representatives of the diplomatic corps, on the great plaza in the outer precincts of the imperial palace in Tokyo.

Yet the analogy with the Arthurian legend should not be pressed too far. Unlike Camelot, the village of Kashihara still exists. The Shinto shrine there – which is called Kashihara Jingu and is served by the Kintetsu company's railway station of the same name – remains a place of pilgrimage for ultra-patriotic right-wing Japanese, many of whom are gangsters or have close links with organised crime syndicates. Moreover, 11 February is still noted in Japanese pocket diaries as National Foundation Memorial Day.

Despite the lingering fantasy in the minds of a few, and all the propaganda which was based on it and which was the source of many of the misconceptions about Japan which persist in the western imagination, the actual history of the world's most enduring dynasty is of great and continuing interest. Serious scholars are agreed that the sovereign line in Japan was actually founded by the most successful among a number of contending local chieftains in the middle to late Yayoi period (c. 100 BC–AD 300). It is my purpose in this book to give some account of the 122 individuals (little more than the names in the case of the legendary first dozen or so) who are said to have preceded the present emperor on the Chrysanthemum Throne (two of them reigned twice), and to suggest reasons for the institution's unique durability. Academic historians, who for the most part deplore the popular interest in genealogy and who often tend to use the word 'antiquarian' pejoratively, will, should they give any thought to it, damn such a hopelessly unfashionable enterprise as a mere catalogue.

It will perhaps be suggested that my 'kings and queens of England' approach is more appropriate to the design of tea-towels for sale in National Trust gift shops than to modern historical writing; and that it was in any case memorably parodied several generations ago by Sellars and Yeatman in *1066 And All That*, with its brisk assessments of monarchs and events associated with them as Good Things or Bad Things.

I am unrepentant, for several reasons, among which perhaps the most significant is that I am by avocation a novelist. As such I am fond of a good story, and have for many years found that of the Chrysanthemum Throne fascinating. In the process of telling it I shall try to show how the role and functions of the emperors have changed over nearly two millennia and how their fortunes have ebbed and flowed. They have been warlords and shamans, high priests, politicians, patrons of poetry and the arts and even deities in human form. The last-named category included, for twenty years, the father of the present emperor, who today is formally described as a 'symbol of the nation' (albeit with some residual priestly duties).

Moreover, I make no apology for basing this book on an essentially chronological plan. The way in which I was taught history as a London schoolboy nearly sixty years ago was no doubt unsatisfactory in many respects. Nevertheless it did at least leave me with a sense of what happened when, and I hope that those interested in things Japanese will find what follows useful as a reference guide to the sequence of historical events, and an aid to relating them to the course of western history. I cannot too strongly stress, however, that I do not set out to write a general history of Japan. That would be impertinent, for there is no shortage of such books, many of them excellent. However, I know of only one other comprehensive account in the English language of the history of the *throne* of Japan, which is an altogether different matter. It was written long before the Second World War, by another amateur. Richard Arthur Brabazon Ponsonby-Fane was a rich and eccentric Englishman with aristocratic connections, who lived for long periods in Japan. Ponsonby-Fane was a fervent believer in the doctrine of the divine right of kings, and an apologist for the unlovely colonial record of pre-war Japan. He was a diligent scholar and a prolific writer, but not a stylish one, alas. Many of his numerous and relentlessly detailed articles about Shinto shrines and the Japanese imperial house were first written for the then equivalent of an in-flight magazine, the travel bulletin of the NYK shipping line. What, if anything, passengers on board NYK vessels made of them can only be guessed at, but they were probably skipped, for they are so paralysingly boring as to be virtually unreadable.

So there is, I believe, room for something more accessible; and this I have tried to offer. I would emphasise that in what follows, social, political and economic issues and developments will be referred to only to the extent necessary to illuminate the lives and experiences of the emperors, empresses regnant and their courtiers. I propose to begin by explaining in this introduction in the form of brief notes the background to a number of commonly used terms, and also to provide information on other relevant matters. First must come the derivation of the very name of the country.

WHY 'JAPAN'?

It was the Chinese who first thought of the islands to the east of their own mainland, in the quarter from which the sun appeared to them each morning, as 'the source of the sun', and began to use the phrase as the country's name. It is represented by two Chinese characters, which the Chinese pronounced as something like 'Ji Pang', which early western travellers corrupted into 'Japan'. The characters are still in official use to represent the name of their country, but are nowadays pronounced by the Japanese as 'Nippon' or 'Nihon'.

WHY 'EMPEROR'?

The Japanese never refer to their reigning sovereign by name, but usually as *Tenno Heika.* This is written with four Chinese characters which are generally translated as 'His Majesty the Emperor'. Literally, *Tenno* means 'Heavenly King'. It should be noted that, until the early nineteenth century, very few westerners were aware of the existence of a sovereign who took precedence over the hereditary shogun. The latter was therefore often described by them as the 'King' of Japan. When the true state of affairs became more widely known, the shogun came to be known by English-speakers as the Tycoon. They called the emperor either the Dairi or the Mikado, the latter term a curiously accurate Japanese version of the expression Sublime Porte. The English word 'emperor' came into general use during the latter half of the nineteenth century, having been approved by Japanese statesmen of the Meiji period, largely, it seems, because there were emperors in Europe. True, the sovereign of Great Britain was a queen, but she soon became Empress of India. The United States had that odd new variety of head of state, a president, which was out of the question for Japan. So it was decided that the sovereign of the new member of the family of nations and contender for international prestige should be called the emperor, for it would have entailed painful loss of face if Japan had a mere king to communicate at the highest diplomatic level with such grandees.

WHY 'CHRYSANTHEMUM'?

The expression 'Chrysanthemum Throne' is also, like so many other ostensibly venerable terms associated with the monarchy, relatively recent. The chrysanthemum flower is native to China. It was introduced into Japan some time in the eighth century AD, and has been prized there ever since for its purity and elegance. The imperial crest, which depicts a double flower with sixteen petals, was adopted officially only in 1889. It is, however, believed to have been used as a personal crest by the emperor Go-Toba, who reigned from 1183 to 1198, and thus has at least the aura of antiquity.

THE IMPERIAL REGALIA

The ceremonially authorised stewardship of the three items which together comprise the regalia is almost the only essential condition of being the legitimate sovereign of Japan. They will be described in detail in the next chapter, for their high significance is rooted in the mythology of the founding of the nation. Briefly, they are, first, the sacred mirror, next the jewel, and then the sword. Of these, only the jewel, which is a piece of polished stone roughly the shape of a three-dimensional comma and (on the evidence of similar jewels found in the tombs of early chieftains) probably about three inches long, is said to be in the personal custody of the sovereign, in a shrine within the precincts of the imperial palace in Tokyo which also contains a replica of the sword. The mirror is believed to be inside the Shinto holy of holies, the Inner Grand Shrine of Ise, while the authentic sword is claimed by the Atsuta Shrine near Nagoya.

The Official List

Though it is now accepted that many of the early names on it are legendary, the list of the occupants of the Japanese throne is to this day approved, maintained and published by the Imperial Household Agency. A separate ministry until 1945, this administrative agency of the Japanese government might best be described for British readers as combining the functions of the Lord Chamberlain and the College of Arms, with some of those of English Heritage. It is a jealous guardian of all matters relating to the throne. The list was last significantly amended (to include Chokei as 98th emperor) as recently as 1926, by command of the then prince regent, who was shortly to become the 124th. Grey areas have not been permitted since a major political dispute arose in 1911 over the status of the five persons who 'reigned' in Kyoto over the so-called northern court during the period of schism from 1331 to 1382. The first four of these are no longer recognised, but the last of them was legitimised as part of the 1382 settlement, and all subsequent sovereigns, including the present emperor, have been of their line.

Genealogical records, whether authentic or otherwise, have all over the world been adduced by those of established or would-be status as justifying their privileged place in society or their claims to one. The English king Edward I claimed a lineage originating in Trojan times, and in our own day the late Lord Mountbatten was notoriously obsessed with what he believed to be his descent from all manner of probable and improbable ancestors. The Japanese had no writing system until Chinese scribes arrived and taught them theirs, but before then powerful people employed oral chroniclers to recite accounts of their antecedents, and it was particularly important for the early leaders of the imperial clan to assert their legitimacy. The first written chronicles of the imperial house were compiled on the basis of these oral traditions at the beginning of the 8th century AD, and were straightforwardly genealogical in style. The first official written list of Japanese emperors dates from that period.

Names

Throughout this book, emperors and empresses regnant are almost always referred to by their *posthumous names*, as they are in the official traditional list. These were not the names by which they were known in life, but were conferred after death, sometimes many years or even centuries later. Buddhist practice in Japan still provides for such names to be given by a priest to a deceased person at the request of the family; cynics suggest that the greater their cash offering, the more resonant the name the priest awards. The present emperor has a personal name, as did all his predecessors, and during his boyhood he was known as Prince Akihito; but only westerners are bold and irreverent enough to refer to him as Akihito now. For the Japanese he is 'the present emperor'. His late father, whom we called Hirohito, is now called 'the Showa emperor', for Showa was the name of his reign. The same formula governed the choice of the posthumous names of his father and grandfather before him. In former times imperial reigns were named more capriciously, and often changed during a single incumbency of the throne. Since the succession of the emperor Meiji in 1867, however, the name of each reign has been announced at its outset, following a complex ritual involving a selection by a committee of scholars and officials from among a limited number of approved Chinese characters. Thus we already know that after his death 'the present emperor' will be called Heisei, and we are living in the Heisei period of Japanese history.

Names of other historical personages cannot be treated with similar consistency, because unlike contemporary Japanese, who are correctly referred to by their family name followed by their personal name, many political leaders of former centuries are today usually identified by the personal name only. Thus Minamoto Yoritomo is almost invariably called simply Yoritomo, Toyotomi Hideyoshi is remembered as Hideyoshi, and the succession of Tokugawa shoguns as Ieyasu, Iemitsu and so on.

It is as if the English were to refer to historical personages by their Christian names alone: Drake and Raleigh, for example, would thus be known as Francis and Walter. In the earliest records prominent people often have the particle '*no*' inserted between the clan name and the personal name, e.g. Soga no Umako. In this usage the particle is equivalent to the German *von* or the French *de.*

The pronunciation of Japanese is not difficult, but many vowels have long and short versions, the former usually being indicated in roman script by a horizontal line above. For simplicity's sake I have used this convention only in the case of the names of emperors, and then just once, when each name appears in capitals as a heading in the text.

EMPRESSES REGNANT

Eight women are officially recorded as having occupied the throne of Japan in their own right, two of them twice; and one other, Jingu, whose name is not on the list, is nevertheless revered and given the courtesy title of empress. Many historians are of the view that one of the first *de facto* rulers of the nation during its formative centuries was a woman known to Chinese chroniclers in the third century AD as Queen Himiko. The last empress regnant was Go-Sakuramachi, who reigned from 1762 till 1771, but did not die until 1813. (The prefix *Go* will be encountered quite often in the names of sovereigns: it means 'after' and is roughly equivalent to 'The Second' in British royal usage.) In 1889 an Imperial House Law was enacted by the new Meiji government, which employed a number of French legal scholars as advisers. Among other changes it provided for the adoption of Salic law, declaring that the succession to the throne might thenceforth pass only through the male line. This rule is now possibly regretted in imperial circles, since neither of the present emperor's two sons has male issue. In the ensuing pages empresses regnant are designated with an asterisk on their first appearance.

CHILD EMPERORS AND ABDICATIONS

Kokaku was the last Japanese sovereign to abdicate. He did so in 1816 after reigning for thirty-six years, but continued to be active in court affairs until his death in 1840. The same law of 1889 ordained that abdication should no longer be a course open to emperors: if the old system had prevailed, the present emperor's grandfather Taisho would almost certainly have been required to abdicate after his physical and mental breakdown, well before his death in 1926.

Yet throughout the greater part of the history of the Japanese throne abdication was a very common practice. No fewer than 60 of the 124 past sovereigns gave up the throne before death (one of these was deposed and two returned to the throne for a second reign). They stepped down for one of three reasons: by their own desire, as a consequence of political pressure, or, most often, because they were too young to have any say in the matter. This third category, of child emperors, reflected the characteristically Japanese taste for governing from behind the scenes at one or even several removes. This may well seem strange, even perverse, to readers familiar with English history and the bibilical warning 'Woe to the land where a child is king'. Had he been a Japanese monarch, Richard III would have done all he could to secure his young nephew Edward V on the throne and rule through him, for a child emperor was very much in the hands of his senior relatives, who might and often did include one or more living former emperors. The maximum recorded tally of former emperors alive at any one time was five.

CLOISTERED EMPERORS

The practice during many hundreds of years was for an emperor to go into ostensible retirement, usually having become a Buddhist priest, but to continue his involvement in the administration 'from the cloister' by setting up a parallel imperial bureaucracy; and many of those who did were political intriguers on a grand scale. Quite how a Shinto 'living god' could have reconciled his divine status with priesthood in an alien religion is one of the many tricky questions which went unanswered during the heyday of emperor worship, and which will be discussed in detail later.

DATES AND AGES

For convenience, all dates are expressed in western terms, BC or AD. In the nineteenth century the western calendar was adopted for most purposes in Japan, though Japanese still generally refer to current dates by reference to the regnal year. In pre-modern times Chinese practice was followed, and all of the earliest dates given in the ancient chronicles are wholly speculative and usually manifestly unreliable. The same adjectives apply to the ages at which emperors and other notables were alleged to have died.

Portraits

The first emperor to be photographed was Meiji, and he was depicted in western-style military uniform. His son Taisho and his grandson Showa were photographed often, in court robes, western-style civilian dress or military uniform, while the present emperor's features are familiar throughout the developed world. Portraits of many of the historical emperors survive, but they are without exception stylised, depicting the subject in court robes or, after abdication, in priestly attire. In only a few of the carved or painted faces is it possible to discern the lineaments of a distinctive individual personality. In the nineteenth century many popular woodblock prints included purported likenesses of members of the imperial family, but they are for the most part as unreliable as they are flattering.

Imperial Consorts

The English word 'empress' used throughout this book conflates a variety of Japanese words, such as *Kogo*, *Chugu*, *Nyogo* and others. These represent different ancient court ranks, which were conferred somewhat arbitrarily upon their recipients in former centuries. The principal consorts of recent emperors have all been given the same, highest rank (*Kogo*), and the old variants are no longer used. Monogamy is a very recent practice for Japanese emperors, Taisho being the first to have had only one official consort. His father Meiji had fourteen children by a number of different consorts, only one of whom was the titular empress (and she not the natural mother of Taisho). The first empress to be photographed (in court robes) was the principal consort of Komei, in the mid-nineteenth century, and her successors have all been photographed, looking very regal in formal western-style gowns. Both the empress dowager and the present empress have been shown not only in court robes and kimono but also in informal western dress.

Imperial Tombs

The oldest imperial tombs which survive date from the Kofun period (AD 300–710). A great many of the elaborate funeral mounds which are characteristic of this period have been traced, clustered mainly in Kyushu and the region formerly known as Yamato, around the modern cities of Osaka and Kobe and in the area to the south of Nara. By no means all of them are imperial tombs, for prominent chieftains of lesser rank were also given funeral mounds. One of the earliest and most impressive has, however, been identified as that of the emperor Nintoku, who is believed to have reigned in the first half of the fifth century. Those of the *kofun* tombs which have been excavated have yielded grave goods of great variety, including evidence of food and drink suggestive of a belief in an afterlife, and a vast number of *haniwa* or unglazed hollow earthenware cylinders or sculptures.

These objects were used from the fourth to the seventh century, and placed not inside but *outside* the funeral mounds, to decorate and symbolically protect them. Some were elaborate, and represented not only human figures but also houses, animals, military or ceremonial objects. Most of the *haniwa* discovered have been between 30 and 50 centimetres high, but a few have been three times as large. In spite of a number of legendary references to the practice, there is no archaeological evidence that living retainers were ever immured in funeral mounds. The imperial tombs or *misasagi* which were constructed in later centuries became progressively less imposing, and the majority of them are very simple and located in austere and modestly sized enclosures. All surviving imperial monuments are maintained and fully protected by the Imperial Household Agency, which prohibits any archaeological investigation.

CHAPTER ONE

Gods, Giants and Methuselahs

Many Japanese words are misleadingly translated into English: none more so than *kami*. It is almost always rendered as 'god' or 'gods', and is indeed used with the honorific suffix '*–sama*' by Japanese believers to refer to the Christian 'God'. However, in ordinary usage, *kami* means both much more and much less, for the word has an extremely diffuse connotation. The great eighteenth-century scholar Motoori Norinaga grappled with it thus:

> I do not yet understand the meaning of the term *kami*. Speaking in general, however, it may be said that *kami* signifies, in the first place, the deities of heaven and earth that appear in the ancient records and also the spirits of the shrines where they are worshipped. It is hardly necessary to say that it includes human beings. It also includes such objects as birds, beasts, trees, plants, seas, mountains and so forth. In ancient usage, anything whatsoever which was outside the ordinary, which possessed superior power or which was awe-inspiring was called *kami*. Eminence here does not refer merely to the superiority of nobility, goodness or meritorious deeds. Evil and mysterious things, if they are extraordinary and dreadful, are called *kami*. It is needless to say that among human beings who are called *kami* the successive generations of sacred emperors are all included. The fact that emperors are also called 'distant *kami*' is because, from the standpoint of common people, they are far-separated, majestic, and worthy of reverence. In a lesser degree we find, in the present as well as in ancient times, human beings who are *kami*. Although they may not be accepted throughout the whole country, yet in each province, each village and each family there are human beings who are *kami*, each one according to his own proper position. The *kami* of the divine age were for the most part human beings of that time and, because the people of that time were all *kami*, it was called the Age of the Gods (*kami*).
>
> (D.C. Holtom, *The National Faith of Japan*, p. 23)

Motoori's illuminating remarks should be borne in mind throughout what follows, most particularly when considering the earliest, legendary accounts of the imperial institution. The 'ancient records' to which he refers are two eighth-century court chronicles, which set out the mythology of the creation of the Japanese nation, and recount the genealogy of the earliest emperors. The *Kojiki*, or Record of Ancient Things, was compiled in 712. It was largely dictated from memory by a court chanter charged with the duty of memorising and reciting the oral traditions of the imperial clan. The *Nihonshoki* (also known as the *Nihongi*), or Chronicles of Japan, was compiled in 720. (About eleven years later on the other side of the world Bede completed his *Ecclesiastical History of the English People.*)

Both of the Japanese chronicle documents are part history, part pure fiction and part propaganda on behalf of those leading families whose prestige and influence derived from reputed descent from certain deities who came to earth from heaven to pave the way for the emperor Jimmu. First among them was Ninigi, the grandson of the sun goddess and ancestor of the first earthly emperor, Jimmu. Of the two accounts, the *Nihongi* was compiled more specifically to reinforce and place beyond dispute the claim of the imperial clan to primacy, and those of the most senior courtiers to their own status. For Ninigi was said to have been attended by a myriad of other deities, and his principal lieutenants among them, each with a specific divine remit, were claimed as the founders of what were to become the aristocratic *uji* or clans. The *Nihongi* is much longer than the *Kojiki*, and it was regarded as being highly suspect by W.G. Aston, one of the distinguished band of British scholar-diplomats whose pioneering work contributed so much to the birth of Japanese studies in the west. Aston made a faithful, meticulously annotated English translation of the *Nihongi* from the original Sino-Japanese. This was first published in 1896, and in his introduction Aston offers the following dismissive comment: 'The earlier part furnishes a very complete assortment of all the forms of the Untrue of which the human mind is capable, whether myth, legend, fable, romance, gossip, mere blundering, or downright fiction.'

The justified implication is that, like the *Kojiki*, the *Nihongi* becomes more valuable as a historical document as it goes on. We are concerned in this chapter, however, with what everybody now agrees to be fiction. It is none the less fascinating and had far more dramatic effects on the Japanese imagination and political developments over the succeeding centuries than the Arthurian legends first promoted by the twelfth-century Welsh bishop, Geoffrey of Monmouth, did in Britain.

The two Japanese chronicles offer slightly differing accounts of the foundation of the country, and of its first, legendary rulers. They agree in asserting that Jimmu was descended from the sun goddess and hence that his line's origins were divine. By the time they came to be written, however, Buddhism had been brought to Japan and had found imperial favour alongside the native polytheistic religion, referred to as Shinto or the Way of the Gods. Before we go further, therefore, it will be well to consider the 'pure' origins of this remarkable amalgam of thought and practice.

Shinto has no scriptures as such, because in its original manifestations it emerged long before the Japanese acquired the art of writing. Indeed the very word 'Shinto' is Chinese, being written with two ideographs, classically pronounced *shin* (god) and *to* (path or way). These characters stand in the native Japanese language for the words *kami-no-michi* which have the same meaning. Shinto was, first, an accretion of rituals and taboos which probably began to be prescribed early in the Yayoi period (300 BC–AD 300). This was when the hunter-gatherer way of life was progressively replaced by a static, agrarian economy based on rice cultivation and which admitted the more elaborate social organisation needed for large groups of people. At first, and essentially, it was necessary to secure the growing crops and thus ensure a bountiful harvest. Rituals designed to propitiate the forces of nature and to protect the people from natural disasters such as earthquakes, fire, flood and pestilence were soon established. The primary act of worship was the symbolic offering of food, and reverence for life manifested itself in fertility rites and the making of images of the male and female sexual organs. (At two popular Shinto shrines in the vicinity of the modern city of Nagoya huge and explicit representations of the vagina and the penis are still respectively the objects of veneration, and are symbolically brought together at a colourful annual festival.)

Shinto is essentially positive, and admits no concept of sin. Its taboos are based on the avoidance of pollution and death, so many of its rituals are concerned with purification. Personal hygiene is crucial, and before worship at a shrine a symbolic bath is taken by rinsing the hands and the mouth with water. Menstruating women should not approach a shrine, and death in a house originally entailed its demolition and replacement. Divinity, as Motoori pointed out, is attributed to natural phenomena such as trees, waterfalls and boulders, which to this day are often protected by sacred ropes and paper talismans, to invite reverence and exclude malign forces.

The mythology elaborated by prominent families to promote and to sustain their dignity and social prestige (for by their own reckoning they were *all* descended from heavenly ancestors) was seamlessly interwoven with the more primitive reverence for and dread of the natural environment to produce a truly indigenous religion. In outline, the Japanese national myth postulates the formation of heaven and earth from chaos and the emergence of seven generations of gods. This culminated in the birth of the god Izanagi and the goddess Izanami, who came together in sexual congress and produced the islands of Japan, the seas, mountains, rivers and trees. Next Izanami bore Amaterasu, a being of such radiance that she ascended to heaven and reigned there as sun goddess, with her first brother the moon god at her side. These primal gods were not unlike those of Egyptian and Greek mythology, in exhibiting a great many all too human characteristics. For example, Amaterasu had a second brother. This was the noisy, bawdy and violent Susano-o, who proved to be so troublesome that his parents sent him to rule the nether world of darkness.

Before doing their bidding, Susano-o went up to heaven, ostensibly to make his farewells, but he so offended his sister Amaterasu by his outrageously coarse and unseemly behaviour that she retreated into the heavenly rock cave, thus casting the world into darkness. Greatly concerned by this development, the myriad congregation of other deities assembled outside, and one of their number contrived to lure the sun goddess from her retreat by performing a lewd dance which so excited her curiosity that Amaterasu emerged to the relief of all. The scapegrace Susano-o, who had by then begotten numerous progeny, was once more banished.

Amaterasu then despatched a number of deities to earth. Two of them entered into negotiations with the earthly chieftain Onanomochi, who was one of the sons of Susano-o, and Onanomochi eventually agreed to cede temporal authority to the sun goddess's grandson Ninigi in return for confirmation of his own primacy in divine matters. The way having been prepared for him, Ninigi in turn descended. This crucial event was described in appropriately solemn terms by the fourteenth-century courtier and historian Kitabatake Chikafusa:

> Then the Great Sun Goddess . . . sent her grandchild to the world below. Eighty million deities obeyed the divine decree to obey and serve him. Among them were thirty-two principal deities, including the gods of the Five Guilds – Ameno Koyane (the first ancestor of the Nakatomi family), Ameno Futodama (the first ancestor of the Imbe family), Ameno Uzume (the first ancestor of the Sarume family), Ishikoridome (the first ancestor of the mirror-makers) and Tamaya (the first ancestor of the jewel-makers). Two of these deities, those of the Nakatomi and the Imbe, received a divine decree specially instructing them to aid and protect the divine grandchild. . . .
>
> Then the Great Goddess, taking in her own hand the precious mirror, gave it to her grandchild, saying, 'When thou, my grandchild, lookst on this mirror, it will be as though thou lookst at myself. Keep it with thee, in the same bed, under the same roof, as [if it were] thy holy mirror.' She then added the curved jewel of increasing prosperity and the sword of gathered clouds, thus completing the three regalia.
>
> She again spoke, 'Illumine all the world with brightness like this mirror. Reign over the world with the wonderful sway of this jewel. Subdue those who will not obey thee by brandishing this divine sword.' It may indeed be understood from these commands why Japan is a divine country and has been ruled by a single imperial line following in legitimate succession.

Chikafusa goes on to emphasise the significance and inspirational quality of the sacred regalia, which were indeed of crucial political importance in the events in which he was himself an active participant. During the recorded history of Japan the regalia, consisting of the jewel and the authorised replicas of the sword and mirror which are in the custody of the reigning emperor, have been the subject of many disputes, to be recounted later. All of the original divinely bestowed items (including the mirror enshrined at Ise and the sword at Atsuta Shrine) are, however, alleged to have survived. Since they are never exposed to human scrutiny, nobody knows what is enclosed within the layer upon layer of silken bags which purport to contain each. The facts give no support to the legend. Metal swords and mirrors were not introduced into Japan, much less manufactured there, until late in the Yayoi period; and the large number of 'curved jewels' (*magatama*) which have been discovered were fashioned at a later date from a variety of materials such as chalcedony, nephrite, jasper, chrysoprase, serpentine, steatite and crystal, some of which do not occur naturally in Japan. The mythical provenance of the sword recalls the legend of Perseus, who in vanquishing the Gorgon employed not only a sword but also used his polished shield as a mirror. There are many references to the supernatural powers of mythical mirrors in western literature, among them Virgil's account of one which extended a ruler's vision, thus enabling him to protect his domains.

In spite of his impressive credentials, Ninigi is not accounted the first emperor of Japan. That distinction belongs to Jimmu, and his name heads the official list. The dates given for the mythological emperors are those of their reputed accession.

1. JIMMU (660 BC)

In 1873 the Japanese government, on the basis of careful analysis by scholars of the chronology implied in the ancient chronicles, declared formally that Jimmu was the first 'earthly sovereign', and that he assumed sovereignty on 11 February 660 BC. (It may be noted in passing that Romulus is said with almost equal precision to have founded Rome in 753 BC.) The principal motive of the oligarchs then in power who instigated this momentous declaration was understandably to provide bedrock for the imperial ideology then being elaborated, and to supply a basis for the associated propaganda (see below, pp. 124–30). There may well also have been a simple desire on their part to gain credit in western eyes, for no European royal house claimed such a long history. The declaration was quite specific about the detail; only the time of day was omitted.

Accordingly, 11 February was designated National Foundation Day, a national holiday, and it was ritually celebrated as such until the end of the Second World War, when it was renamed National Foundation Memorial Day.

The description of Jimmu in the *Nihongi* conjures up a picture of a middle-aged, campaigning general, adept in using dirty tricks, leading an army of bloodthirsty ruffians addicted to raucous singing in the manner of English football supporters in the late twentieth century. At the age of 45 Jimmu became aware of the call of destiny and assumed the mantle of statesmanship. This is what the *Nihongi* claims he said to his followers at that time:

> From the date when our heavenly ancestor descended until now it is over 1,792,470 years [*sic*]. But the remote regions do not yet enjoy the blessings of Imperial rule. Every town has always been allowed to have its lord and every village its chief, who, each one for himself, makes division of territory and practises mutual aggression and conflict.

The site of Jimmu's supposed tomb near Mount Unebi

Having therefore brought the sacred regalia to a palace (a flimsy structure with a raised floor) which he had ordered to be erected at Kashihara in Yamato, Jimmu conducted ceremonies in honour of the sun goddess and was proclaimed emperor of Japan. His coronation was the culmination of an epic journey which he was said to have undertaken from a starting point on the coast of Kyushu. After proceeding along the shores of the Inland Sea, pacifying or defeating the tribes encountered on the way, Jimmu at length reached and subdued the Yamato region, the heartland of the Japanese nation. Having formally become emperor, Jimmu granted the title of empress to the wife he had acquired a year earlier, ceremonially visited various parts of his realm, and made a number of grants of land to his principal lieutenants, during a reign of suitably amazing length: no less than seventy-six years until he died at the age of 127. From 1873 until 1945 an imperial envoy was sent annually on 3 April to the spot north-east of Mount Unebi officially recognised as the site of the founding emperor's tomb, bearing offerings of products of mountains, rivers and the sea.

2. SUIZEI (581 BC)

At the time of Jimmu's death three of his sons survived. One of them was already a centenarian, but after joining in the mourning for their father he began to plot the downfall of his younger half-brothers. Learning of this they agreed that he should be put to death, and a special bow and arrow were prepared with which to kill their venerable senior. A good opportunity presented itself when he was asleep and alone, but the elder half-brother's nerve failed him at the last minute and Suizei did the killing. Thereupon the timid (and much smaller) one acknowledged forthwith Suizei's claim to succeed (the chronicles do not say whether or not the giant was still brandishing the bow at the time) and at the age of 48 Suizei became the second emperor. Among other women he married his aunt, who bore him a child, and according to the *Nihongi* he died aged 84. Neither he nor any other emperor until Sujin is given a death date in the *Kojiki*, and this fact, combined with the dearth of anecdotal material about them in either chronicle, has given rise to the hypothesis that the earliest 'emperors' whose names alone are given below represent a long period of political instability and of shifting alliances among rival families also claiming descent from Ninigi rather than from the other deities in his retinue. Certainly the detailed accounts of the credentials of numerous consorts are indicative of creative genealogical efforts on the part of the compilers, intended to bolster the position in the court pecking order of certain other aristocratic families. The accession dates (BC) given in brackets beside each name are those set down in the *Nihongi.*

3. ANNEI (549)
4. ITOKU (510)
5. KŌSHŌ (475)
6. KŌAN (392)
7. KŌREI (290)
8. KŌGEN (214)
9. KAIKA (158)
10. SUJIN (98)

The chronicles are much more forthcoming about the tenth emperor, Sujin, whose posthumous name means 'honouring the gods'. It was perhaps chosen because of the great pestilence which is said to have ravaged the country in the fifth year of his reign, resulting in the deaths of half of the population. The survivors 'took to vagabondage, and there was rebellion, the violence of which was such that by worth alone (that is through the virtues of the sovereign) it could not be assuaged'. So Sujin offered himself to the gods for punishment; and after a protracted period of divination and a number of prophetic dreams, learned that they were displeased by being worshipped collectively. Accordingly, Sujin (who functioned as chief priest as well as ruler) gave detailed instructions for the dedication of particular shrines to particular deities, and delegated to suitable families the duty to furnish hereditary priests to minister to them. A lucky man called Ikuhi from the village of Takahashi was appointed Brewer to the Great Deity (of grain crops), and celebrated by presenting sacred *sake* to Sujin and singing a song to him. Things took a turn for the better at once, and it was considered that the time had come to give some attention to the 'barbarians' who lived outside the area where the imperial writ ran.

In his capacity as general, Sujin directed a number of military campaigns, described in the *Nihongi* in bloody and earthy detail (the enemy soldiers were so terrified that they soiled their trousers) which is in sharp contrast to the stately Chinese style which characterises much of the genealogical material. Sujin is stated to have lived to the fabulous age of 120, or even possibly 168.

11. SUININ (29 BC)

The chronicles have it that during the reign of Suinin, the third child of Sujin, formal contacts were made with emissaries from Korea. The reign was eventful: Suinin survived a plot by the elder brother of one of his consorts to have her assassinate him, and in a triumph of optimism over experience took a great many other wives and concubines. Much of the power of the early emperors was derived from their role as shamans, and the prophetic dreams they experienced in that capacity. People believed in them implicitly (and not only in Japan, as the Old Testament bears witness). Following one such dream, Suinin arranged for the sacred mirror, the most important of the three items of the imperial regalia, to be enshrined in perpetuity in what is now known as the Naiku, one of the two grand shrines at Ise. He also appointed one of his daughters to be the resident priestess-guardian there. Early Shinto rituals were partly shaped by practices originating in Korea and brought at about this time to Japan by way of Izumo on the Japan Sea coast, site of another surviving grand shrine. Suinin was the first recorded patron of wrestling, and on the recommendation of his favourite champion is said to have ordered the substitution of the clay images called *haniwa* for living retainers in imperial burial rites. (It has been pointed out in the Introduction, p. 11, that archaeological evidence has not been found to support the notion that human sacrifices of this kind were ever in fact made in Japan, though they undoubtedly were in China and elsewhere.)

12. KEIKŌ (AD 71)

The third son of Suinin, Keiko was, like his ancestor Suizei, described as being of gigantic physical stature, and a victorious warrior. His son Yamato Dake, a national hero to this day, is credited with having torn to pieces one of his brothers, who had offended their father. After this bloody demonstration of filial devotion Yamato Dake went on to lead expeditions to Kyushu and to subdue rebellious 'barbarians' there before proceeding to regions north and east of modern Tokyo to confront the Yemishi (the indigenous Ainu people, of Caucasian origin, who were over the centuries progressively driven from the main island, Honshu, and into the northernmost island of Hokkaido, where a very few survive). After recounting further heroic exploits and masterstrokes of deception, the legend tells of Yamato Dake's death on the return journey. The emperor Keiko is recorded as having begotten seventy-two sons and eight daughters, and to have died at Shiga in Omi, east of modern Kyoto, which he made his capital towards the end of his life.

13. SEIMU (AD 131)

Seimu was a son of Keiko, and was credited with the appointment of the first provincial governors and district officials. Seimu had one son, who seems to have died young, because after this emperor's death the succession passed for the first time to a nephew (Chuai, whom Seimu had made crown prince in the forty-eighth year of his reign). His chief minister, Takeuchi, served five emperors and either lived to be over 300 years old or, more credibly, was in fact several men with the same name who succeeded one another in the office. The chronology proposed in the eighth-century records is wildly imaginative, but it seems likely that a settled bureaucracy did develop as soon as the imperial clan's primacy was established beyond dispute.

14. CHŪAI (AD 192)

Chuai is believed to have established and maintained his capital in Kyushu for several years, after proceeding there to quell yet another rebellion; and it is entirely likely that such an expedition did in fact take place, but several hundred years later. Chuai died in battle and was succeeded by his widow, the warrior heroine Jingu, still referred to as 'empress' though her name is not enrolled as such on the official list. Chuai was described as a phenomenally big man, like his grandfather Keiko.

It should be borne in mind that imaginative tales about national prehistory are by no means unique to Japan. Nor are claims to divine ancestry. Alexander the Great was accorded divine status in about 300 BC, and it became common for Roman emperors to apotheosise themselves. Christians to this day worship a Jew born in Palestine two thousand years ago as the son of God. For people such as the early Japanese chieftains, who could and did conceive of a hierarchy of divinities, there was no illogicality in agreeing, even if they did so with some reluctance, to recognise the sovereign primacy of one clan even while insisting that they and their children were also descended from the gods.

CHAPTER TWO

Shaping a Monarchy

The eighth-century chronicles make beguiling reading, but we must look elsewhere for more reliable information about the earliest period of Japanese imperial history: to the archaeological record, and to early Chinese chronicles. Together these support the thesis that the first rulers of a consolidated Japanese state emerged from two groups of tribes, both of Mongol stock. One of these settled in Kyushu, and pushed into Yamato by way of the Inland Sea between the mid-third and mid-fifth centuries. Yamato is the area known today as the Kansai region, around the cities of Osaka, Kobe, Kyoto and Nara, and which includes the Kii peninsula; it gives its name not only to the heartland of Japan but also to the dominant ethnic group of its population. The second tribe settled in and developed the area around Izumo on the Japan Sea coast. Its members were more advanced culturally than those of the Kyushu group; and the different emphases found in the mythological accounts of the origin of the Japanese nation given in the first two chronicles reflect their respective sources.

Evidence of early political organisation is provided by written Chinese records dating from the Wei dynasty of the third century AD, which refer to tribute offered by 'the people of Wa' (an early name for Japan still in use in certain contexts) to 'the people of Yen', which was a kingdom in China. These writings also refer admiringly to a queen called Himiko, who may have been the first *de facto* woman sovereign of Japan, and was said to rule over 'one hundred countries' (communities). It is further stated that, when Himiko died, a male prince aspired to succeed her but was rejected by the people, who chose in his stead a girl of thirteen called Iyo or Ichiyo. There is also evidence of very early 'official' contacts between Kyushu and Korea.

The 'countries' referred to by the Chinese scribes were upwards of a hundred clans or very extended families (*uji*), which by early in the sixth century formed a loose ascendancy presided over by a dominant kinship group which became the Japanese imperial family. They seized rights over developed land and constituted the aristocracy, the head of each *uji* claiming descent from a different Shinto deity, and the head of each family unit within the clan exercising a priestly function. Some of the clan chiefs in a close relationship with the 'imperial' *uji* enjoyed hereditary ranks and positions at court, and some exercised power comparable with or even superior to that of the first emperors. They may well, therefore, have nourished ambitions to dislodge them, and the fact that the chronicles lack anecdotal material, however fanciful, about eight of the 'emperors' from Suizei onwards almost certainly reflects a period of political turbulence during which rival tribes and warlords contended for dominance.

What is certain is that, until the beginning of the sixth century, the emperors of Japan were still essentially warlords, and that they ruled both by the sword and with the support of Shinto rituals which also gave status and dignity to other chiefs of clans. Clan affiliation was not exclusively by way of blood relationships: territorial ties were also involved. The contents of the large stone chambers surmounted by huge earthen mounds (*kofun*) in which the bodies of clan leaders were placed during this period afford some clues as to the manner of their lives. It may be inferred that the many swords, mirrors and polished stone jewels discovered were emblems of authority, since the same three items comprised the imperial regalia. The most important Shinto shrines in Japan, those at Ise and Izumo, were also established during this period. The activities of the early emperors seem to have centred on combat, hunting, feasting and drinking. Animal flesh was certainly an important part of the imperial and aristocratic diet: it was not until Buddhist missionaries with vegetarian inclinations arrived that meat came to be frowned upon. The eating of fish was always permitted to those who could afford it, and wild boar meat continued in favour under the polite fiction that it was derived from a creature known as the 'mountain whale'.

The transition from legend to more or less reliable history cannot be dated with precision, but we are on progressively surer ground as to the facts if not the exact dates when discussing the fifteenth sovereign and his successors. It should again be stressed that the ages at which some of them are reputed to have died are particularly suspect.

15. ŌJIN (270)

Ojin ascended the throne in AD 270 according to tradition, but is now thought to have reigned in the late fourth to early fifth century. He was the son of Jingu Kogo, Chuai's formidable widow, who was not only a successful general and clever diplomat but also functioned as a shaman and priestess. As Ojin's guardian, Jingu may have exercised imperial powers for a time, though the office of regent did not then exist. During Ojin's reign there was a significant amount of traffic between Japan and China (via Korea), and some Korean historians argue that Ojin was in fact himself a Korean. The learned Chinese scribe Wan'i is believed to have been welcomed at the imperial court. Wan'i may well have instructed the emperor in the Chinese language: it is known that Chinese was adopted by the Japanese court in the time of Nintoku, Ojin's successor. The Japanese vernacular was until then relatively pure and spoken by all. The introduction of Chinese led to the progressive creolisation of Japanese and the importation of polite variants and Chinese constructions, which accelerated as the ideographs with which Chinese is written – totally unsuitable for the purpose – were pressed into clumsy service as an improvised script for the native language. The Chinese language was also the means of introducing members of the imperial circle to Confucian thought, which was to shape the forms and accidentals of future government.

After his death, Ojin was apotheosised as Hachiman, god of war, and became the tutelary deity of countless Shinto shrines all over Japan. This singular distinction should probably have gone instead to his gallant mother, who went into battle in an advanced state of pregnancy and emerged victorious. There was no reason why a woman should not have been raised to the pantheon: after all, the principal Shinto deity, Amaterasu, was female. Nevertheless, it was to the spirit of Jingu's son that petitions for success in battle were addressed throughout the succeeding centuries, up to and including the Second World War.

16. NINTOKU (313)

According to tradition, Nintoku ascended to the throne in 313 after a complex succession dispute, but he is now thought to have died in about

AD 400. During his reign silk was introduced into Japan from Korea; and though there was as yet no cash economy, villages inhabited by those who tilled the land, worked forests or fished were subject to heavy taxation in kind, including unpaid agricultural labour. The *Nihongi* relates that, in the fourth year of his reign, Nintoku was struck when surveying his domains from a high tower by the absence of smoke rising from the dwellings of the common people. He correctly deduced that they had no rice to cook, and was so perturbed by the knowledge that he decreed that, for the space of three years, the rule providing for forced labour was to be suspended. He fully accepted the less than agreeable personal consequences for himself and his family:

> Therefore the palace enclosure fell to ruin and was not rebuilt; the thatch decayed and was not repaired; the wind and rain entered by the chinks and soaked the coverlets; the sunlight filtered through the decayed places and exposed the bed-mats. After this the wind and rain came in due season, the five grains [rice, millet and other crops] produced in abundance. For the space of three autumns the people had plenty, the praises of his virtue filled the land, and the smoke of cooking was also thick. . . .

Having noted for himself this evidence of the satisfactory and popular results of his initiative, Nintoku made what might strike modern readers as a distinctly smug speech to his empress, impressing upon her that the people's poverty was the prince's poverty, and that their prosperity was likewise his. Afterwards he presumably gave instructions for the commoners to resume the corvée and undertake the overdue refurbishment of his own quarters and those of his entourage.

However, the emperor's marriage was heading for the rocks. Powerful and forthright women abounded in Japan in pre-Confucian times, and Nintoku had married one. His principal consort was of comparatively humble birth, but he nevertheless respected her enough to have appointed her formally to be his empress. She emerges from the chronicles as a person of considerable force of character, who objected strongly and repeatedly when Nintoku mentioned to her on a number of occasions that he was minded to introduce his younger half-sister into the household as a concubine. Determined to have his way, Nintoku seized an opportunity provided by the absence of the empress, who was visiting Kii, to install the girl in his palace. When she learned of this *fait accompli*, the empress chose to live elsewhere, and though Nintoku went personally to appeal to her to accept the situation, she never returned to him.

What is claimed to be Nintoku's 'keyhole' funeral mound near Osaka (his palace was in nearby Naniwa) is, at more than 480 metres in length (far more extensive than the ship burial at Sutton Hoo), the biggest in Japan. Its construction must have entailed great cost in labour and materials. The interior of the tomb was explored in the early Meiji period by at least one westerner, an Englishman called William Gowland who was employed at the newly established mint in nearby Osaka; but since the 1880s the Imperial Household Agency has adamantly refused access to it to scholars and others alike, and has needless to say forbidden its excavation. It remains a prominent landmark; and its contents are a tantalising mystery to all except the deceased Mr Gowland and those who constructed and furnished the tomb so long ago.

17. RICHŪ (400)

Nintoku's successor Richu reigned for only five years, early in the fifth century, having emerged victorious from a dispute with a rival candidate. In the fourth year of Richu's reign 'local Recorders were appointed for the first time in the various provinces, who noted down statements, and communicated the writings of the four quarters [every part of the empire]': an indication that literacy in Chinese was by then becoming more widespread. An imperial treasury was formally established in Richu's time, with responsible accountants (possibly some of the Korean immigrants who formed part of his entourage) under a senior courtier who had control of 'gold and silver, jewels, precious utensils, brocade and satin, sarsnet [a fine silk], rugs and mattresses, and the rare objects sent as tribute by the various barbarians'. The mattresses referred to were the precursors of the *tatami* mats which gradually came into use to cover the entire floors of rooms in respectable Japanese dwellings. Richu's death was attributed to a disease caused by lack of harmony in the 'elements of water and earth' in his body: a diagnosis revealing that Chinese medical and yin and yang theories had already been introduced into aristocratic circles in Japan.

18. HANZEI (406)

Fantasy returns in the sketchy accounts of Hanzei, a brother of his predecessor Richu. Hanzei was yet another sovereign reputed to have been endowed with most unusual physical characteristics. He is said to have been over nine feet tall and to have had enormous teeth, all of the same size. In spite or perhaps because of Hanzei's daunting appearance, the country enjoyed tranquillity and prosperity during his six-year reign, and Hanzei died peacefully in his palace.

19. INGYŌ (412)

He was succeeded by one of his younger sons, who ascended to the throne with great reluctance, perhaps because, unlike his father, he was no superman. Ingyo is indeed the first emperor to be openly described as physically disabled, suffering from some kind of paralysis of the legs. The story goes that, happily, a skilled physician from Korea was able to cure the emperor's disability. The delighted Ingyo rewarded the man liberally before sending him back to his own country and enjoying his restored fitness. In his euphoria he fell in love with the younger sister of his empress. He installed her in a separate palace and, now able to get about, frequently visited her. During his reign, Ingyo devised an ingenious plan to arrest and indeed reverse the proliferation of the titles of nobility which had been assumed over the years by ambitious families. Ingyo decreed that all holders of dubious titles who wished to have them confirmed should undergo a public ordeal, by plunging their arms into boiling water or mud, with the assurance that if they were genuine they would be magically preserved from harm. Not surprisingly, many bogus titles were quietly shed. Ingyo's private life, like those of so many of his predecessors and successors, was complicated by continual domestic quarrels, but he is nevertheless said to have been a centenarian when he died.

20. ANKŌ (453)

Ingyo's death opened a particularly bloody chapter in the history of the imperial house. His successor Anko killed his own father, the heir presumptive, in order to gain the throne, but reigned for only two years before retribution was meted out to him when Anko was 56. He was lying in a drunken stupor one day with his head resting in the lap of his favourite consort, when his nephew the young prince Mayowa, at the reputed age of seven, exacted revenge for the earlier murder by decapitating him.

21. YŪRYAKU (456)

The imperial family seems to have produced so many spectacularly bloodthirsty criminals at this time, whose exploits became the stuff of enduring legend, that one may reasonably suspect that it was a period of civil war. Yuryaku, who succeeded his brother Anko in 457, is described even by the court's own chroniclers (who may have wanted to contrast him with the mild and virtuous twenty-third emperor Kenzo) as a 'greatly wicked' man, who had placed himself in line for the throne by murdering or arranging the killing of nearly all the other eligible candidates. If, on the other hand, the many stories of Yuryaku's depravity and wanton cruelty are credited, he seems to have been the Japanese Caligula.

22. SEINEI (479)

Seinei was Yuryaku's son, and, perhaps understandably in view of his antecedents, his hair was reputed to have been white from birth. He is said to have reigned from 479 until 484, and his other noteworthy characteristic was a dislike of dogs, horses and 'playthings', which people were by decree forbidden to offer to him. After his death there was an interregnum owing to a lack of qualified candidates, a consequence of Yuryaku's murderous activities. But then, in a twist on the story of the virtuous Roman dictator Cincinnatus, two surviving grandsons of the emperor Richu were discovered. They were living as simple herdsmen in a remote area, whence they were escorted back to the capital. Both showed a sensible reluctance to occupy the vacant throne, and for about a year each repeatedly declined the honour and offered it to the other. Meantime it was left to their sister, the princess Oshinumi-no-Iitoyo-no-ao, to administer the government as regent.

23. KENZŌ (485)

Kenzo was the younger of the two rustic princes, and at length he agreed to accept the dignity of emperor. Unfortunately he died at the age of 38, without issue, two years after ascending to the throne. This was a matter of general regret, according to the chroniclers who, living early in the eighth century, were much influenced by both Confucian and Buddhist notions of virtue in statesmen. They stressed that the widespread grief for the passing of the emperor was because, having known poverty himself, Kenzo had been renowned as a just, compassionate and kindly ruler of his people during his brief reign. He was nevertheless consumed with hatred for the memory of the late emperor Yuryaku, and asked his elder brother, now the crown prince and soon to become the emperor Ninken, to go and demolish Yuryaku's tomb. The crown prince made a show of obeying his younger brother, but in fact inflicted only minor, token damage on the old reprobate's last resting place.

24. NINKEN (488)

Kenzo's principal widow, who had twice publicly slighted Ninken during the reign of her husband, committed suicide when he in turn became emperor. Ninken chose a daughter of Yuryaku to be his empress, which may account for the perfunctoriness of his defacement of her late father's tomb. She bore him one son and six daughters. At the time of Ninken's death in 498 the country was described as prosperous and the people content.

25. BURETSU (498)

This emperor died childless, and with him Nintoku's line came to an end, perhaps mercifully. For if Yuryaku was the Japanese Caligula, Buretsu was undoubtedly their Nero, being like the Roman emperor an amateur vivisectionist. The chronicles say nothing good about him: he was well versed in the law and took a keen personal interest in the infliction of physical punishment. A voluptuary and a sadist, he 'ripped up the belly of a pregnant woman and inspected the pregnant womb . . . and plucked out men's nails, and made them dig up yams. . . . He made men climb up trees and then shot them down with a bow, upon which he laughed.' So similar is Buretsu's reported character to that of his predecessor Yuryaku, indeed, that some scholars have argued that the two were in fact one and the same man, the three intervening occupants of the throne being either completely fictitious or temporarily successful rebels during Yuryaku's reign.

However that may be, a new potential focus of political power was created with the emergence at about this time of a clan which branched off from the imperial line itself. It took the family name Soga, and its successive heads, possibly as a reward to the first of them for agreeing to a political bargain, gained an influential hereditary place at court, as quartermasters and treasurers. This provided a springboard for the further advancement of their descendants. The dates set forth in the official list are more reliable in the case of Buretsu's successors and the duration of each reign is given in brackets after each name.

26. KEITAI (507–31)

The new emperor, a descendant of Ojin the fifteenth emperor, was also reluctant to succeed. He ascended the throne when already middle-aged, and must have come as a great relief to his courtiers, because 'he loved the people, and was courteous to men of worth. He was of a generous disposition.' He married a daughter of the emperor Ninken, and took in addition eight concubines, all of whom are named in the *Nihongi*. Keitai was the first emperor formally to abdicate, though his reign was barely truncated by this act, since he was reputed to be aged 82 and on his deathbed at the time.

27. ANKAN (531–6)

Keitai was succeeded by his elderly son Ankan, who if we are to trust the chronicles, must have been born when Keitai was himself only 13. Ankan reigned for five years before dying, childless, at the age of 70, to be succeeded by his younger brother, Senka.

28. SENKA (536–9)

Until Ankan's time, the evidence suggests that the emperors ruled as well as reigned. The leaders of the Soga family were, however, by then firmly entrenched as the first full-time senior court bureaucrats, much to the disgruntlement of two other prominent aristocratic families. These were the Mononobe, who furnished the imperial guard, and the Nakatomi, the hereditary ritualists. Both, needless to say, claimed divine descent.

The series of dual systems of government which characterised the political history of Japan for nearly fourteen hundred years may be said to have been initiated when the emperor Senka appointed Iname, head of the Soga clan, as his executive first minister. Iname thus became an authorised power in the land, and his successors, as heads of the clan, inherited his position as mayor of the palace and effective ruler of Japan. The transmission of Buddhism to Japan was first to challenge but eventually to consolidate their position.

29. KIMMEI (539–71)

Senka's successor Kimmei was also a son of the emperor Keitai, but he had been passed over previously on account of his youth. Significantly, he took as consorts two of Iname's daughters. It was during the reign of Kimmei that an event of crucial significance for the subsequent political and cultural history of Japan took place. The king of Kudara in Korea sent to the emperor as gifts an image of the Buddha and some Buddhist scriptures. Interested by these exotic curiosities, and aware that they related to an alien religion which he had certainly heard about from Chinese and Korean visitors, Kimmei consulted his ministers about what should be done with them. His minister Iname recommended that the new religion should be tried out, while, not surprisingly, his rivals the heads of the Mononobe and Nakatomi clans were opposed; the latter especially, in his capacity as the hereditary chief custodian of Shinto and its official ritualist. As a compromise, Kimmei gave the image and scrolls to Iname, instructing him to worship them by way of an experiment. Iname did so, but to his chagrin his efforts were almost immediately followed by a pestilence which afflicted the people. This disaster not surprisingly resulted in a serious setback both to Soga prestige and to that of Buddhism; but it was temporary only.

30. BIDATSU (572–85)

The second son of Kimmei, Bidatsu reigned for three years from 572. The even more formidable Sogo no Umako succeeded his father Iname as first minister, and the power struggles at court over Buddhism continued as more scriptures, images and even priests and nuns arrived from Korea. The introduction of Buddhism had a profound impact on the native system of beliefs and worship. From the first its appeal for emperors created a paradoxical situation, since they were *ex officio* Shinto high priests and shamans, authorised (like the popes as vicars of Christ on earth) by means of ritual acts to mediate with the deities, though not themselves at that time considered to be divine in the sense that westerners use that term. Flirtation with Buddhism clearly imperilled their very legitimacy, but proved to be dangerously attractive and eventually irresistible. Bidatsu remained ambivalent, wavering between Buddhism and the native religion until he fell victim to the pestilence himself at the age of 47.

31. YŌMEI (585–7)

Yomei was a half-brother of Bidatsu, and during his short reign he formally embraced Buddhism. He was the first emperor to do so, and the long-term significance of his decision cannot be too strongly emphasised. At this stage, Buddhism had manifested itself in Japan as the exclusive pursuit of the literate: it was a matter of copying sutras and other texts, and the performance of ritual ceremonies of the most arcane nature. The apotropaic potential of Buddhism was not neglected: it was thought to be 'superior' to Shinto not only in the refinement of its liturgy but also because its aristocratic adherents believed that, in spite of Soga no Iname's disastrous early experiment, the Buddha could outperform the native deities in protecting the nation from famine, pestilence and other disasters. Immigrant Buddhist priests were socially acceptable on account of their erudition, and they and their Japanese students and successors were soon to constitute the first meritocracy. After Yomei paved the way and most subsequent occupants of the throne adopted the new religion, imperial patronage transformed the higher ranks of the priesthood into a network where preferment was largely a matter of 'connections'; a situation similar to that which prevailed in the Anglican establishment in England in the eighteenth and early nineteenth centuries. Yomei is notable for a second reason. He was the father of the great Shotoku Taishi (see 33 below) by his own half-sister, who was one of his consorts.

32. SUSHUN (587–92)

Yomei's successor Sushun was a nephew of Soga no Umako, and Umako engineered his selection by defeating in an armed struggle an attempt by Moriya, by then head of the Mononobe clan, to promote an alternative candidate. Despite owing his elevation to his pro-Buddhist uncle, Sushun is known to have been opposed to the new and alien religion, and to have begun to plan to dislodge Umako from his position of ministerial dominance. It is a measure of the personal power of the head of the Soga clan that, when apprised of this plot by one of the palace women, Umako forthwith ordered the emperor's assassination, and had him buried without ceremony on the day he was killed. Sushun was 73 when he met his violent death.

33. SUIKO* (593–628)

At the time of Sushun's assassination a number of eligible male candidates for the succession were available, but Umako (who went on to order the murder of two of them) installed his niece, a sister of the emperor Yomei and widow of Bidatsu, as the first empress regnant. One of the tokens of office given to her was the imperial seal, which had already by then come into use. Seals as such were not a novelty and they confirm the existence of a burgeoning bureaucracy. The oldest which has so far been found in Japan was unearthed by a farmer in Kyushu in 1784. Made of gold, and

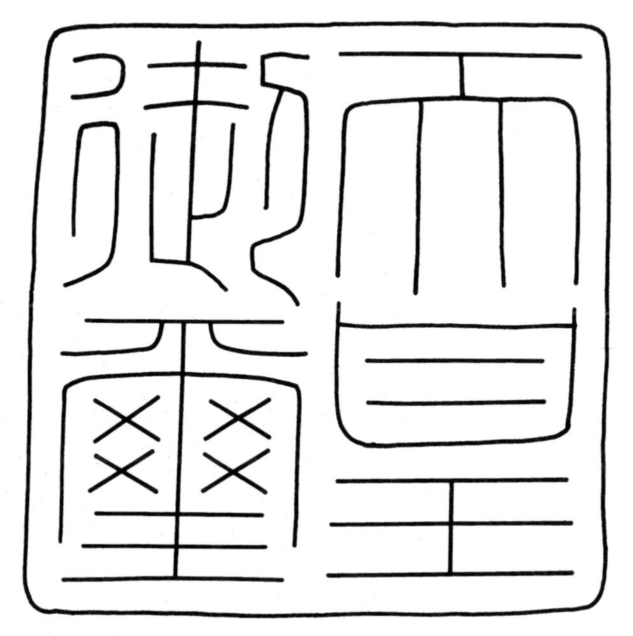

Impression of the imperial seal

beautifully fashioned in the Chinese style, it bears an inscription indicating that it was presented to the ruler of the 'state of Na of Wa' by the emperor Guangwa of the latter Han dynasty and a date equivalent to AD 57.

The successful installation of the empress Suiko confirmed that the Soga clan was now politically supreme, and Umako's own designs on the throne became ever more obvious. It was during Suiko's reign that the Chinese word *Tenno* was imported and used to refer to the sovereign, who had previously been described as *Okimi* or 'first among equals'. It enhanced the status of the throne, for the *Tenno* alone was qualified to preside over rites invoking the sun goddess Amaterasu, who had by no means been sidelined by the advance of Buddhism. No doubt in response to the challenge of the imported creed, Shinto itself was becoming more sophisticated by absorbing elements of Confucianism and the theory of yin and yang. These accretions were to become central to the philosophy which supported the imperial institution in particular and the national polity as a whole. The doctrine that the *Tenno*'s formal stewardship of the sacred regalia was essential to his or her legitimacy was formalised during Suiko's reign.

All this did not mean that the empress herself exercised powers commensurate with her prestige. Her nephew the prince Umayado (Shotoku Taishi) was installed as crown prince. To Umako's dismay he proved, as Suiko's regent, to be more than a match for the incumbent minister. Indeed Shotoku Taishi was the effective ruler until his death at the age of 49 in 621. A devout Buddhist and an accomplished scholar, Shotoku Taishi was renowned as having been an infant prodigy who could speak at birth, while in maturity he was said to have had the enviable capacity of attending to the petitions of ten men simultaneously. He ordered the construction of the surviving Horyu-ji temple not far from modern Nara, and its Yumedono (pavilion of dreams) was the site of the prophetic dreams for which he is still remembered.

Shotoku was also a far-seeing statesman and lawgiver, who was much impressed by what he had learned from immigrant advisers about Chinese institutions and court protocol, and resolved to introduce them to Japan. Accordingly he transformed and regulated the practices at the empress Suiko's court, organising the nobility into an elaborate hierarchy with appropriate robes and insignia prescribed for each rank, and planned and established a centralised administration. The disgruntled Umako outlived him but himself died in 626, two years before his niece the empress.

34. JOMEI (629–41)

Shotoku Taishi had a son, who seems to have inherited some of his father's talents and was available to succeed Suiko. But Shotoku was dead, and his immense influence was a thing of the past. The Soga star was no longer eclipsed, and Soga no Emishi, who was now head of the clan and had inherited his father Umako's ministerial post, ignored Shotoku's heir and installed his preferred candidate Jomei, a grandson of the emperor Bidatsu. Jomei was the puppet of his minister throughout his reign.

35. KŌGYOKU* (642–5)

On the death of Jomei there was a male heir apparent, but Soga no Emishi and his son Iruka, who were by then in total control of court affairs, preferred to elevate to the throne the prince's mother, Jomei's widow. During her first, three-year reign, the arrogant pretensions of the Soga family so incensed their main rivals the Nakatomi clan that Kamatari, its head, entered into a conspiracy with the imperial prince Naka, who was later to become the emperor Tenji, to bring about their downfall. In due course they staged a spectacular and successful coup d'état at a court ceremony to receive envoys and accept tribute from Kudara in Korea. Soga no Iruka was killed, in the presence of the empress, while Kamatari sent troops to deal with Iruka's father Emishi in his house. Emishi, accepting that the Sogas' long ascendancy was finally at an end, personally set fire to the house, and he and his attendants perished in the flames.

36. KŌTOKU (645–54)

In the aftermath of the literal destruction of the Soga house after a century of effective dominance challenged only by Shotoku Taishi, the empress Kogyoku sent for her son prince Naka, Kamatari's ally, and proposed to abdicate in his favour. This move had been foreseen by Kamatari, on whose advice the prince declined, agreeing that his mother should abdicate but suggesting her brother Karu rather than himself as her successor. Karu duly reigned as the emperor Kotoku, appointing Naka to be crown prince. With his ally Kamatari, Naka took over the reins of government and instituted the so-called Taika reforms.

This radical reorganisation based on T'ang Chinese models involved the setting up of a provincial administrative system with stipendiary officials, and the organisation of a census and a land survey. The next step was to allot cultivated areas to the peasants who worked them on an 'equal-field' basis which took account of variations in productivity, with special allocations to provide income for the imperial household, aristocrats and officials according to their status. Individual peasant households were taxed on the produce of their fields as well as being liable for levies of cloth and labour.

At the same time the central government apparatus was augmented by two new departments: the *Jingikan* or office of Shinto worship, and the *Ommyoryo* or bureau of yin and yang divination. Their respective functions were to regularise and prescribe the seasonal pattern of ritual Shinto ceremonies, and to practise and refine the techniques of divination associated with the Chinese Confucian tradition as an aid to political decision making. Kamatari's own Nakatomi clan, in collaboration with the Imbe and the Urabe, assumed responsibility for regulating Shinto, while two other aristocratic clans, the Abe and the Kamo, were appointed to specialise in divination.

37. SAIMEI* (655–61)

Kotoku having died at the age of 59, the politically active crown prince declined to succeed him in what he saw as a more restricting role, and reinstalled his mother the former empress Kogyoku on the throne. She reigned for a further seven years under the name of Saimei. A tough and gallant woman, she joined the crown prince when he mounted a military expedition to assist the king of Kudara who had appealed for help, but became ill and died on active service at Chikuzen at the age of 67.

38. TENJI (668–71)

Her son the crown prince then at last succeeded to the throne as the emperor Tenji. However, he remained politically active in alliance with Kamatari until his death. As a sign of his gratitude to his old comrade in arms and trusted lieutenant, Tenji favoured him with the grant of a new family name, Fujiwara. Kamatari thus ceased to belong to the Nakatomi clan of which he had been the head, and founded a new dynasty destined for political greatness and enduring influence (it produced prime ministers until the middle of the present century). His career illustrates the remarkable continuity of certain families – often assisted, it is true, by the judicious adoption of suitable sons-in-law and other promising males – which has characterised Japanese society throughout its recorded history.

Tenji and his brother Temmu after him were without much doubt the most genuinely powerful sovereigns in the history of Japan. Their assumption of dictatorial authority was expressed in Confucian terms as representing a mandate from heaven. They elevated members of their family to all key ministerial posts, and their own status to a degree which ruled out the possibility of a successful challenge by any other claimants to the throne except one, and he was soon disposed of.

39. KŌBUN (671–2)

This was Tenji's favourite son, who did in fact succeed his father, as the emperor Kobun. The posthumous name of this sovereign was not conferred until 1870. Then the government of the emperor Meiji arranged, as part of its campaign to establish the bona fides of the new political regime, for the official list of the previous occupants of the throne to be carefully scrutinised, and for authorised amendments to be made. Kobun's reign lasted a few months only, and was as unhappy as it was brief. For the impatient Temmu fomented an armed rising, known as the *jinshin no ran,* and challenged his nephew. Kobun took the field in person against him, but was defeated in battle and committed suicide.

40. TEMMU (673–86)

Tenji's brother then seized the throne, in effect by force of arms, claiming the triumph of Confucian virtue as his justification. Temmu was an inveterate intriguer, and once installed as emperor he covered his political flanks against potential rivals by taking nine carefully chosen and well-connected wives. Four of these were his own nieces (Tenji's daughters), two were daughters of Fujiwara Kamatari, and one was a Soga. Temmu was unfriendly to Buddhism, and as an active patron of Shinto he initiated the custom, which is still in force, of rebuilding the grand shrines at Ise every twenty years as a symbol of rebirth and affirmation of their perpetuity. Temmu's interest in the native religion, its mythological origins and its significance for the throne prompted him to order the compilation of written historical records of imperial history, hitherto transmitted orally. He may, therefore, justly be described as the man responsible for the creation of the official list of emperors in which his defeated predecessor was to be included more than a millennium later.

41. JITŌ* (690–7)

Despite all Temmu's artful planning to secure the future of his line, none of his sons succeeded him: one of them was indeed executed for attempting prematurely to seize the throne. Eventually his principal widow, one of the nieces he took to wife, was installed as the empress regnant Jito. She was assisted by the new crown prince, a son she had had by a different man, until his own death in 689. In that year the empress gave instructions to her provincial governors that one in four able-bodied male peasants should be trained as soldiers; this was the first known provision for conscription in Japan. Jito's reign ended in 697, when she abdicated in favour of her grandson; and on her death six years later she was the first sovereign whose body was cremated in the new, Buddhist fashion.

42. MOMMU (697–707)

Because he had been nominated in her lifetime by his formidable grandmother, Mommu broke with tradition by becoming the first minor to ascend the throne (when he was 14). He died while still only 25. His principal consort, whom he is unlikely to have been permitted to choose for himself, was a Fujiwara, early evidence that the new clan founded by Kamatari was already influential at court. The young emperor did leave a son, but on the early death of his father this boy prince was passed over in favour of his grandmother, and had to wait for a good many years before his own eventual elevation.

43. GEMMEI* (707–15)

Mommu's mother, Gemmei, was a half-sister of the late empress Jito. Until the reign of Gemmei it had been the practice for each occupant of the throne to establish a new capital. This apparently extravagant course of action was a consequence of the traditional Shinto doctrine that death occurring in a house polluted it. Such a momentous death as that of a sovereign was, by extension, held to pollute all the buildings associated with the court; but since the structures concerned were flimsy, far from durable in any case and occupied a relatively small area, it was not particularly expensive to start afresh on a different site. But Gemmei, like many of her entourage, was struck by the tales she had heard of the grandeur of the courts of China. Envious, and persuaded that the revenues of her now efficiently administered government were sufficient to fund the work, she ordered the construction of a spacious city designed to be a permanent capital, and moved there in 710. This was Nara, which was then known as Heijo-kyo; and the city did remain the capital, with only one brief interruption, until 784. Gemmei renewed the emperor Temmu's instruction that an official, written history should be compiled, and the *Kojiki* was completed in 712. Gemmei abdicated at the age of 54 in favour of her daughter, and died seven years later.

44. GENSHŌ* (715–24)

The daughter of Gemmei and a granddaughter of Temmu, Gensho inherited an already sophisticated administration, but sought to improve it by ordering a revision of the Taiho code of 710. This resulted in a comprehensive formulary which specified the functions and laid down rules for all government officials, and it remained technically in force until the nineteenth century. Among other provisions, the code authorised the use of four types of seal to guarantee the authenticity of documents. First in importance was the imperial seal, then came that of the *Dajokan* or grand council of state. Next in status were the seals used by senior officials in government departments and bureaux, and finally those of the provincial governors. All produced impressions in vermilion ink. They were needed. Throughout the Nara period, government was mostly by the reigning sovereign, acting through chief ministers and a very large national bureaucracy recently estimated by Japanese scholars to have numbered as many as ten thousand officials. All of these were in theory meritocrats, but in practice they owed their positions largely to family connections.

During Gemmei's reign the second great historical chronicle, the *Nihongi* or *Nihon Shoki* was completed. It recounted the national history up to the abdication of Jito in 697, and like all official documents of the Nara period it was written in classical Chinese, so was accessible only to a very few.

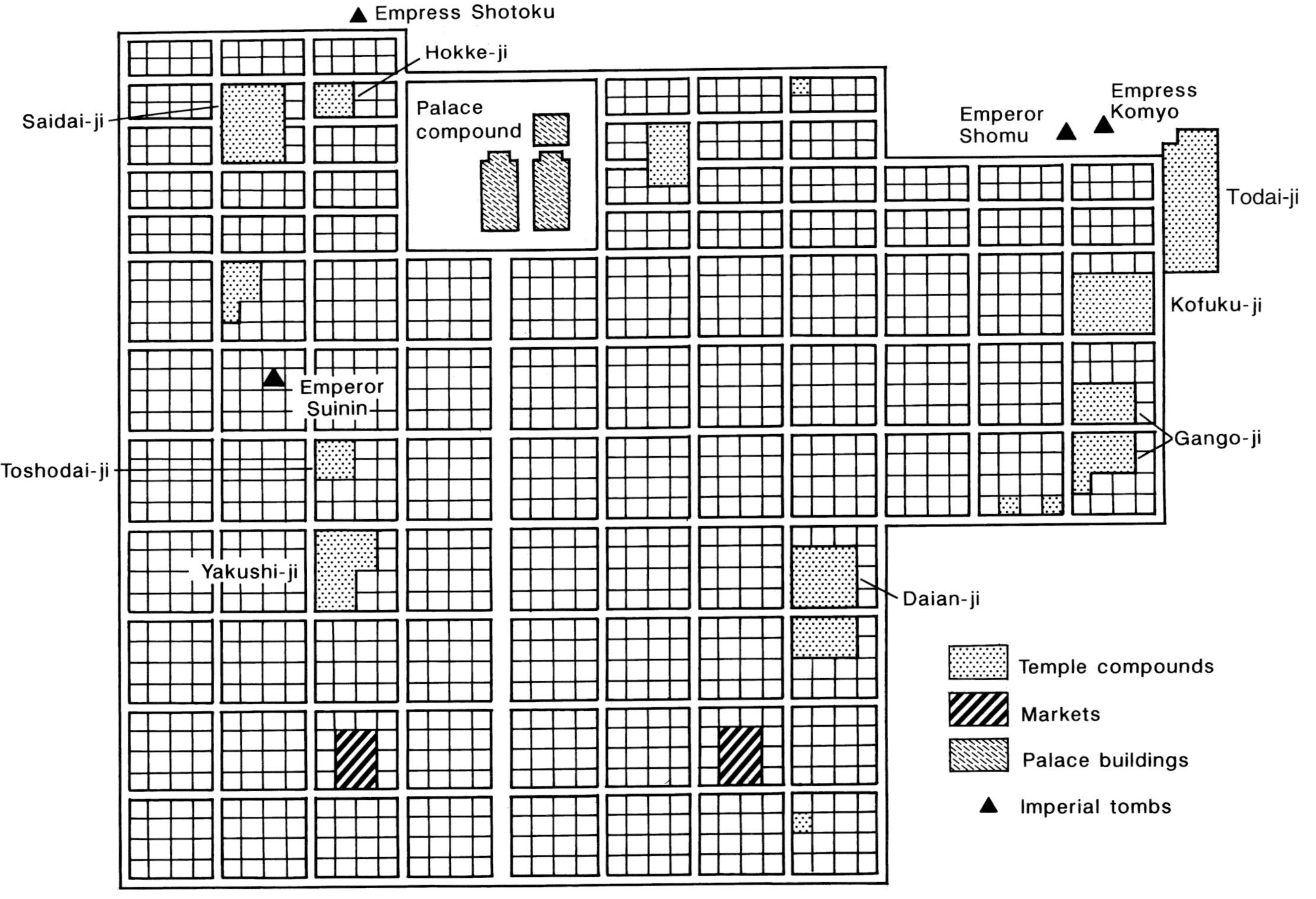

Heijo-kyo (Nara), founded in AD 710 and seen here as it was in the latter half of the eighth century

45. SHŌMU (724–49)

Shomu was the son of Mommu who had been deemed too young to succeed at the time of his father's death, but he was now elevated by Gemmei, his aunt, who abdicated in his favour when he was 23. Shomu was a fervent Buddhist, being much influenced by the learned and charismatic priest Gembo. He ordered the construction of a monastery and a seven-storey pagoda in every province, and conceived the idea of casting the gigantic image of the Buddha which is still to be seen in the Todaiji temple in Nara. During his reign another priest, Gyoki, with Shomu's support, originated and promoted the theory that the native Shinto deities were avatars of the Buddha. This doctrine of *Ryobu-Shinto* had enormous influence, not least because it addressed the anomalous position of an emperor who was a pious Buddhist but retained many ritual duties as the supreme priest and sole intermediary of the Shinto sun goddess Amaterasu. Apparently on a whim, Shomu briefly moved his capital to Kuni, but returned to Nara two years later, and in 749 he relinquished the throne in order to become a monk. After his death seven years later, Shomu's widow Komyo presented to the Todaiji temple in Nara a huge collection of objects and artefacts used by the former emperor in his lifetime. It included furniture, ceramics, weapons, medicines from China, textiles, a five-stringed lute, masks, and a board for playing the game of *Go.* They were and are still housed in a wooden building elevated a few feet from the ground and known as the Shoso-in. In outward appearance it somewhat resembles a log cabin. That it still fulfils its original function after well over a thousand years is not due to neglect on the part of the authorities of their duty to care for such irreplaceable treasures. Quite the contrary: the Shoso-in has provided ideal conditions for the long-term storage of its contents in darkness and at a stable temperature. Selected items from the Shoso-in collection are very occasionally transferred to museums for brief public exhibition.

46. KŌKEN* (749–58)

Shomu was succeeded by his unmarried daughter, who reigned as the empress Koken. She was also a keen if not personally devout Buddhist, who lavished funds on the construction and adornment of temples. She was a susceptible woman who became the mistress of her minister Fujiwara no Nakamaro and entrusted matters of government to him. So pliant was she that in 758 Nakamaro persuaded her to abdicate in favour of Junnin, a grandson of the emperor Temmu. Possibly Koken welcomed abdication as a convenient way of ending her affair with Nakamaro, because though she became a nun she soon took another lover, and thereby the involvement of the former empress in the affairs of the imperial household actually increased.

47. JUNNIN (758–64)

Koken's new liaison was with a politically ambitious Buddhist priest called Dokyo. Unsurprisingly, Dokyo incurred the hostility of his predecessor in her affections, and when the priest purloined the imperial seal, which had been in Koken's possession, Nakamaro, now confusingly called Oshikatsu, attempted to raise troops to attack him. He was, however, defeated and then executed. Claiming that the emperor must have been a party to the move against her lover, Koken dethroned Junnin and exiled him to Awaji, where he was strangled soon afterwards. Not until 1871 was he given his posthumous name of Junnin, and enrolled as the forty-seventh emperor in the official list of sovereigns of Japan.

48. SHŌTOKU* (764–70)

The former empress and sexually adventurous Buddhist nun now reascended the throne, reigning as Shotoku and piously stating that she considered her duty 'first to serve the Three Treasures [the Buddha, the Buddhist Law and the Buddhist community], then to worship the [Shinto] gods, and next to cherish the people'. In practice she showered honours on her favourite, the priest Dokyo, who openly lived under the same roof as the empress, while plotting to seize the throne for himself. He almost succeeded in persuading his mistress to abdicate in his favour, but was frustrated by Kiyomaro, the new head of the Fujiwara clan. Shotoku retaliated by sending Kiyomaro into exile, but before the persistent Dokyo could make another move the empress died, and his game was up.

49. KŌNIN (770–81)

A grandson of the great emperor Tenji, Konin was already 62 when he became emperor in 770, but lived on for more than eleven years. His signal achievement was to sort out the mess he inherited by banishing the troublesome priest Dokyo and recalling Kiyomaro from exile, making him his senior minister. Konin thereafter enjoyed a relatively tranquil reign, and abdicated a few months before his death.

CHAPTER THREE

Vision and Extravagance at the Imperial Court

The acceptance of Buddhism into Japanese culture as offering a parallel and (since unlike Shinto it came with an impressive scriptural apparatus) possibly superior mechanism for the invocation of divine protection from plague, famine and other disasters and the exorcism of vengeful or otherwise unwelcome spirits did not as we have seen proceed without challenge. However, it attracted imperial interest from the outset and, later, patronage in varying degrees; and on the whole was welcomed as an additional rather than an alternative source of support. To this day in traditional family homes, prayers and petitions are commonly offered at a miniature Shinto shrine or 'god-shelf' and at a domestic Buddhist altar in the same house, depending on the context. For ordinary Japanese, imbued with the Chinese yin and yang philosophy, it makes good sense to turn to Shinto which is essentially Yang, or positive, and pray for success in such matters as birth and marriage, education, and new initiatives and challenges, while it is regarded as the preserve of Buddhism with its Yin or darker, more negative, aspects to deal with sickness, death, the honouring of deceased ancestors, and with troubles of every kind.

Buddhism was later to develop populist appeal for the Japanese people, but it was initially fashionable among the literate upper classes, with profound social and economic consequences as the priesthood became an established and esteemed profession. By the middle of the eighth century Nara was not only an impressive imperial capital. With its plethora of wealthy temples and influential priests, it had also become a stronghold of the new religion, which constituted a political force to be reckoned with. The fiftieth emperor rose to the challenge.

50. KAMMU (781–806)

By common consent one of the four or five greatest sovereigns who have occupied the throne of Japan, Kammu – believed by some modern historians to have had a Korean mother – had been appointed crown prince at the mature age of 39 by his reluctant father the emperor Konin, who, no doubt with an eye to enjoying a long and influential retirement, would have preferred to see his daughter Sakahito succeed him, or, failing her, another of his sons. As crown prince, Kammu had been given oversight of the Chinese-style imperial 'university', where both the sons of noble courtiers and potential senior bureaucrats were instructed in the Chinese language and its literature (and hence were much influenced by Confucian doctrines).

During his young manhood Kammu had observed the steady progress of Buddhism and the accretion of economic and political influence to its clergy in Nara; to such an extent that the city had become a virtual theocracy and, as he saw it, a threat to the status of the imperial institution itself. On ascending the throne in 781, therefore, one of Kammu's first acts was to decree that a new and even more magnificent capital city should be planned and constructed. The first site to be chosen was at Nagaoka, well to the north of Nara; but this soon proved unsatisfactory, and a fresh start was made some distance away to the east. Kammu's new imperial seat was to be called Heian-kyo, and much of its original layout as well as street names survive in its modern-day manifestation as Kyoto.

The topography of the new site was highly satisfactory from a practical point of view, being at the confluence of two rivers. It was also warmly recommended by the court geomancers, since the unpropitious north-easterly approaches (whence evil spirits were and are thought to come) were physically protected by the bulk of Mount Hiei. It is an irony of history that as soon as the city began to take shape, Buddhist temples were constructed near the summit of Mount Hiei, ostensibly to add a spiritual barrier to that provided by nature. These temples formed the basis of the great Enryaki-ji complex of the Tendai sect. This esoteric form of Buddhism was brought to Japan by the monk Saicho (767–822), who founded the Enryaku-ji and boldly designated it as a 'Centre for the Protection of the Nation'.

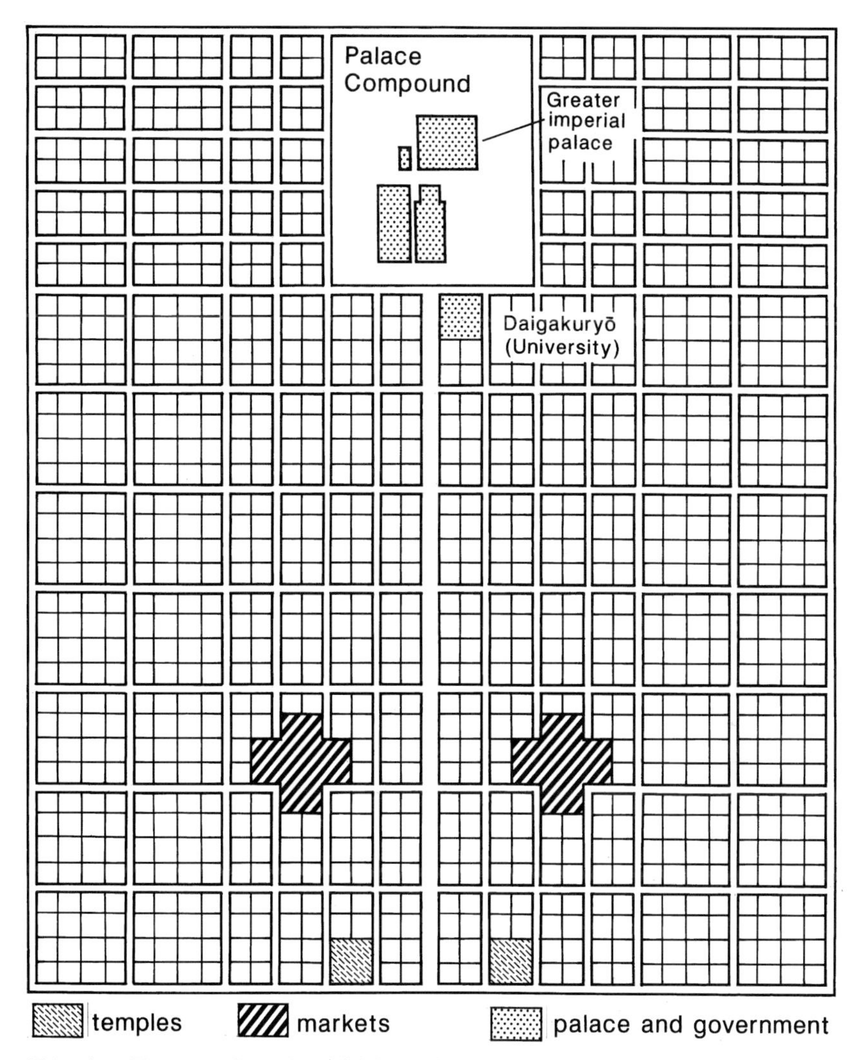

Heian-kyo (Kyoto) as planned in 794, but only partially developed

The former capital city was not simply abandoned and virtually forgotten in the way that other imperial capitals had been: Nara was too monumental and richly endowed for such a course to be conceivable. It remained a sizeable and sophisticated city which prospered, as it has to this day, as an important religious, commercial and cultural centre. Nara was nevertheless dwarfed by its successor Heian-kyo, for Kammu's imperial base was created on an enormous scale. As Nara itself had been, the city was laid out on a grid pattern derived from Chinese models. Its western and southern districts were not developed until modern times, but the central, northern and eastern parts of Heian-kyo closest to Mount Hiei flourished. From late medieval times until 1868 when the imperial court moved to Edo, which was designated as the new Eastern Capital (the literal meaning of 'Tokyo'), Heian-kyo was usually called Miyako. Since then it has borne its present name, Kyoto or Capital Metropolis. The city suffered much physical damage and was indeed at one stage virtually laid waste, but it was always rebuilt, and it remained the imperial capital of Japan through both tranquil and turbulent times for over a thousand years. It was also the site of the flowering of a culture of wonderful refinement and complexity.

Massive buildings for imperial and official use were constructed of wood, lacquered in vermilion and roofed with ornate ceramic tiles in the Chinese style. The principal part of the present Heian Shrine in Kyoto, which was built in the nineteenth century on a site near the middle of the city, is a two-thirds scale replica of Kammu's palace, and it conveys a vivid impression of the grandeur of the emperor's vision. The structures erected for private domestic use by the nobles and high officials of the imperial court were in sharp contrast. They were simple and austere, being made of unpainted wood and thatched with many layers of strips of bark rather than roofed with tiles. A typical mansion of this kind consisted of an interconnected series of pavilions with elevated wooden floors, placed around a central garden with a stream as its focus. Little privacy was afforded by the bamboo or paper screens behind which the high-born women of such houses passed most of their lives.

A strong and decisive ruler enjoying the economic security which the efficient national taxation system provided, Kammu was assisted throughout the quarter-century of his reign by able ministers whom he never allowed to dominate him. It was Kammu who in 794 commissioned the first *Sei-i-tai-shogun* or 'Barbarian-quelling Great General'. This military title was at a later stage to describe the office of the head of the civil government of Japan. Originally, however, and for a long time afterwards, a shogun held a strictly temporary appointment for the duration of a campaign, usually against unruly Yemishi (Ainu) tribesmen in the north-east of the country.

The emperor was not only a man of political vision and a decisive administrator: by disposition he was a scholar who devoted a good deal of time to the study of the classics and to the promotion of Chinese studies generally. He had an elevated view of his status, and a keen sense of the past and potential continuity of the dynasty. It was Kammu who ordered one of his ministers, Omi no Mifune, to select a posthumous name for each of his predecessors on the throne. His numerous consorts reputedly bore him a total of thirty-six children, the eldest of whom became crown prince and succeeded him.

51. HEIZEI (806–9)

This was Heizei, whose accession to the throne was disputed by one of his brothers, the future emperor Saga. Heizei, an amiable man who had inherited some of his father's scholarly gifts but not his talent or taste for government, decided after three years on the throne that he would abdicate in Saga's favour. His expressed willingness to retire greatly displeased his principal consort, Fujiwara no Kusuku, who had aspired to the formal title of empress and could not reconcile herself to the evaporation of her prospects. A determined woman, Kusuku took the extreme course of fomenting an armed rising with the sole object of reinstating her husband as emperor. It was put down by forces loyal to Saga, and Kusuku, disgraced, committed suicide. The retired emperor Heizei became a priest and withdrew from the stage completely, to live on in retirement for another fourteen years.

52. SAGA (809–23)

Saga was, like his brother, an accomplished Chinese scholar, renowned as one of the three finest calligraphers of his time. He also took a keen interest, as his father Kammu had done, in the arrangements for the formal education of young scions of the aristocracy. His personal tastes were hedonistic and he lived in spendthrift luxury, making ends meet in the short term by selling grants of tax-free land, which of course reduced the recurrent revenues of the imperial family and later entailed serious financial difficulties for his successors. He was reputedly the first emperor to have tasted tea, when he accepted a cup from a Buddhist priest in 815. Saga had nearly fifty children and, unable to meet the huge expense of maintaining them all in imperial style, lowered the status of his seventh and subsequent sons to that of ordinary subject. This was a stratagem first devised by his father, and one which was to be employed by several subsequent emperors. The sons who were effectively disinherited by Saga were given the new family name Minamoto, which was to resound in later Japanese history in its own right. Saga appointed another of his brothers to be his crown prince and heir apparent, and abdicated in his favour after fourteen years on the throne. He then retired to live out his remaining years in the western suburb of Heian-kyo which is still called Saga in his memory. His impressive palace there eventually became the headquarters of the senior branch of the imperial family and, much restored and adapted, survives as the present Daikaku-ji temple.

53. JUNNA (823–33)

Saga's successor Junna resembled the two brothers who preceded him on the throne in both temperament and tastes, so his financial position was also precarious. During his reign centralised imperial government still functioned, though with less efficiency, and further attempts were made to bring remote areas under administrative control (and incidentally to enlarge the government's shrinking tax base). One of the most important imperial edicts fixed the number of provinces at sixty-eight, which total included the two major islands now called Kyushu and Shikoku, an administrative arrangement which was to continue in force for more than a thousand years. A new department of government was also set up, to deal with disciplinary and criminal matters.

In spite of these measures, the personal extravagances of emperors who lived so conspicuously beyond their means led them to go on mortgaging the revenues and thus systematically weakening the power of the throne. It may be wondered what they found to spend so much money on; there is after all only so much one can eat and drink, and although vast quantities of *sake* were consumed, the court's diet was hardly of gourmet quality.

Imperial progresses and pilgrimages involved massive expenditure, however, and the finest silks and precious *objets d'art* were routinely exchanged as gifts. Life at court became more and more inward-looking, and the business of government, still theoretically by the emperor through the elaborate bureaucracy, was during the reign of Junna's successor Nimmyo to become a shadowy matter of power broking dominated by the Fujiwara clan (which as we have seen was founded by a former head of the Nakatomi family). Senior courtiers continued to be appointed to ostensibly political offices with impressive titles, but they were sinecures. Generations later the Fujiwara ascendancy was itself threatened by descendants of the imperial offspring who had, in order to save expense, been disinherited. During Junna's reign the great military house of Taira was founded by one of Saga's nephews, and the elements were in place for the eventual civil war in which the Taira were pitted against the Minamoto as bitter rivals, even though the leaders of both clans were of imperial blood. Junna abdicated in 833 in favour of one of Saga's sons, and died seven years later.

54. NIMMYŌ (833–50)

On ascending the throne, Nimmyo recognised an obligation to his uncle, and sought to discharge it by his selection of a crown prince. This was Junna's son Tsunesada. Tsunesada was, unusually, not the child of a Fujiwara mother, and Nimmyo by choosing him not only angered his own sons (he had fifteen) but also the formidable Fujiwara family which interpreted the nomination as an attack on their access to the innermost imperial circles. Nevertheless Nimmyo obstinately tried to sustain the awkward arrangement, which led to complex internecine squabbling. Ultimately he failed: the crown prince was deposed and, with his two sons, renounced public life by entering the Buddhist priesthood. When Nimmyo died his own eldest son Montoku, whose mother was a Fujiwara, became emperor.

55. MONTOKU (850–8)

During Montoku's reign the political dominance of the Fujiwara family, which was to endure for two centuries, was established beyond question.

The Emperor Montoku

Fujiwara Yoshifusa was not only the new emperor's uncle but also his father-in-law, and Yoshifusa now arranged to have himself appointed chief minister as well. Montoku was a puppet emperor, who was subsidised in a life of luxury by the immensely wealthy Fujiwara clan. He seems to have occupied himself mainly in the women's quarters of his palace, for by the time of his death at the age of 31 he had begotten twenty-seven children. One of his sons became the next emperor, Seiwa.

56. SEIWA (858–76)

Seiwa was only nine years old when he succeeded his father, and Yoshifusa, as the boy's maternal grandfather and grand panjandrum at court, at once added the title of regent to his already impressive collection; he was the first person not of imperial blood to occupy the post. He then arranged for the boy-emperor to take as consort one of his nieces, Takaiko, an experienced woman who knew what was expected of her and in due

Montoku's empress, Somedono

course bore Seiwa a son. Her service in the Fujiwara cause earned her the formal title of empress, with the name Somedono. In order to enhance Somedono's dignity, her former lover, the poet Narihira, was banished from court and advised to enter the priesthood. The emperor was still a young man when he was freed from Yoshifusa's oppressive proximity by the master intriguer's death in 872, but his new liberty of action did not seem to suit him, and he abdicated four years later at the age of 26, becoming a monk. Seiwa is reputed to have been an exceptionally handsome man, like his famous later kinsman the warrior chieftain Yoritomo, though Heian period notions of male beauty would probably strike most Japanese today as being distinctly odd. An almost perfectly round, white face and a smooth, hairless complexion were regarded as the ideal in a man of high birth.

57. YŌZEI (876–84)

Yozei, Seiwa's son by his mature Fujiwara empress Somedono, was ten years old when he succeeded his father. Another Fujiwara, Mototsune (the adopted son of the late Yoshifusa) assumed the regency. As he grew to manhood, it became apparent that the character of the young emperor was deeply flawed. He was ungovernable and criminally violent, his excesses including the murder of the son of his former wet-nurse; and it was Mototsune who was responsible for ejecting him from the throne when he was 18. Yozei did not go quietly: as a retired emperor he had to be treated with honour, and his person remained sacrosanct. No doubt to the surprise and disappointment of all who had to attend upon him, he lived on for more than six decades, terrorising his acquaintances and neighbours until nearly the end. Shortly before his eventual death at the patriarchal age of 82 Yozei became a priest, though last-minute repentance and a tranquil end were never claimed for him.

58. KŌKŌ (884–7)

The throne now being to all intents and purposes in the gift of the Fujiwaras, the delinquent youth Yozei was succeeded by his sober great-uncle, aged 55 and the third son of the emperor Nimmyo. He was reputedly the father of forty-five children, most of whom had been demoted and taken the name of Minamoto, but at that stage Mototsune saw Koko as a stopgap, keeping the throne warm for one of the princes who were more closely related to Mototsune himself but had to be bypassed on account of their extreme youth. Less than four years later, however, Koko became fatally ill, and the most senior court officials including Mototsune had to face the immediate problem that no crown prince had been nominated. An unprecedented ruling was made. Koko's 21-year-old seventh son Sadami, who had been stripped of his imperial status and was by then a Minamoto, was as a matter of urgency readmitted to the imperial family and appointed to be crown prince on the day before Koko's death. Sadami duly succeeded his father, as the emperor Uda.

59. UDA (887–97)

Uda had to accept Mototsune as his chief minister, but after the latter's death in 891, Uda demonstrated his independence of spirit by disregarding the claims of Fujiwara candidates and instead appointing an erudite outsider to be his principal counsellor. This was the meritocrat official Sugawara Michizane, the last of the Chinese-style bureaucrats to rise so high. The origins of his family were humble, but his grandfather and father before him had achieved eminence in the academic sphere as professors of literature at the university and consequent attachment to the imperial court and senior rank. Having been his father's ablest pupil, Michizane followed in his footsteps and became one of the only two professors (the other presiding over Chinese studies). Being primarily a poet and scholar, he was admirably suited to academic life, but as a member of the bureacracy he had to serve in any post to which was appointed. In 890 he returned to the capital after acting for a year with a good deal of reluctance and no great distinction as governor of the province of Sanuki (the present Kagawa prefecture) in Shikoku.

Uda admired Michizane, and welcomed him to his side, adding injury to the insult to Fujiwara pride by accepting Michizane's recommendation that no further embassies should be despatched to China. This was not as dramatic a diplomatic volte-face as it might seem; such missions were in any case in virtual abeyance, having for a long time been at best sporadic and often postponed. Nevertheless, this evidence of the new man's influence on the emperor offended the Fujiwara grandees, which in turn gratified Uda. Under the false impression that he had bested them once and for all, Uda abdicated in 897, nominating his thirteen-year-old son to succeed him. He then entered the priesthood, becoming the abbot of the Zen Buddhist temple of Ninna-ji in north-east Kyoto, and assumed a novel title, that of *Ho-O* or cloistered emperor. As such, Uda intended to become a power behind the scenes, manipulating the new emperor himself, but his ambition was largely unfulfilled.

60. DAIGO (897–930)

When Daigo succeeded his father he inherited Michizane, not only as his principal minister but also as his tutor, and as such the most influential

The Emperor Daigo

politician in the land. Michizane retained a foot in the academic world, and intervened unnecessarily in various scholarly disputes. This was to the advantage of the leaders of the Fujiwara camp, who were determined to destroy Michizane, and mounted a campaign of slander against him. Having fabricated and avidly circulated rumours of his disloyalty, Michizane's rivals persuaded Daigo to sign a decree which consigned his adviser and teacher to a provincial appointment in Kyushu. Outraged when he learned of this, the former emperor Uda went in person to the imperial palace to lodge a protest, but he was, unprecedentedly, denied admission. To underscore further their authority, the Fujiwara had Michizane demoted from his already demeaning post at Dazaifu near Fukuoka in north Kyushu, where he died from malnutrition at the age of 59, protesting to the last his loyalty to the throne.

But that was very far from being the end of Sugawara Michizane. His death was shortly followed by those of a suspicious number of prominent people known to have been hostile to him, as well as several natural disasters, including a bolt of lightning which struck the imperial palace. All these events were represented to Daigo as the work of Michizane's unquiet spirit. In the face of Fujiwara protests, the unnerved emperor ordered the posthumous rehabilitation of his former tutor. Michizane's reputation having been restored, the whole affair became something of a popular focus for anti-court sentiments among people at large, and the late statesman was within a few decades of his ignominious death given the highest posthumous distinction, when he was declared to be a Shinto deity. As such he is still worshipped and petitioned at thousands of shrines all over Japan as Tenjin, patron of scholarship and inspiration to examination candidates.

In spite of this setback, in the absence of an alternative centre of effective political power in the capital, on Daigo's own death the ascendancy reverted to the Fujiwara. His successor Suzaku, who was just eight years old when he ascended the throne, was placed under the tutelage of a Fujiwara regent in the person of Tadahira, the new head of the clan.

61. SUZAKU (930–46)

Tadahira lacked the devious political skills of his wily predecessor Yoshifusa, and was indecisive in the face of two serious rebellions which took place during Suzaku's reign. One of them was fomented by a pretender to the throne, Taira no Masakado, who actually proclaimed himself emperor and established a short-lived alternative court, before being attacked and killed by a Fujiwara general. Suzaku had a daughter but no son, so he appointed his brother Nariakira, subsequently the emperor Murakami, to be crown prince two years before abdicating in his favour.

62. MURAKAMI (946–67)

Accounted an amiable man, a talented poet and a music-lover, Murakami decided after the death of his minister Tadahira to take up the reins of government personally, but his aspirations were not matched by ability or decisiveness. Most historians agree that it was during Murakami's reign that central government became so weak and ineffective and the Fujiwara so obsessed with their need to control the imperial family that other great military houses in alliance with neglected and disgruntled provincial governors filled the power vacuum which had formed at a regional level. Vast private estates had made the Fujiwaras immensely wealthy, and the 'equal-field' principle, never fully implemented for peasants, broke down completely in the frenzy of land-grabbing by locally powerful families. Crippled by taxes, many peasants gave up their holdings and migrated to undeveloped areas; but, as new land was opened up, the Fujiwara-dominated court squandered its advantage by giving grants and exemptions on a lavish scale to nobles and to fashionable Buddhist temples.

In outlying provinces where any pretence of central administration had been abandoned, prominent families had recourse to arms to protect themselves and their dependants. Those in the south-west tended to accept Taira hegemony, while those in the north-east acknowledged the authority of the Minamoto. The aristocracy therefore became divided between the Kyoto-based civil nobility, who were still attached to the Fujiwara as a fount of patronage at court, and their military counterparts in the provinces, whose allegiance was essentially geographical.

These alignments had little direct impact on the increasingly artificial world of the imperial court, where questions of the succession continued to be of most concern and harsh reality intruded only occasionally, as when in 960 the imperial palace built by command of the emperor Kammu two hundred years earlier was destroyed by fire. Just before his death Murakami, knowing that the health of his eldest son the crown prince was precarious, nominated his third son to be the next emperor but one.

63. REIZEI (967–9)

Though in fact he lived in quiet valetudinarian retirement to the age of 61, Murakami's successor Reizei did have a weak constitution. He struggled through the prescribed accession ceremonies with the utmost difficulty, and abdicated less than two years later, in 969.

64. EN'YŪ (969–84)

In spite of the emperor Murakami's expressed wish that his third son should be the next in succession, En'yu, a younger son then aged only ten, was installed in 969, with the year-old infant son of Reizei named as crown prince. The children were of course dominated by their Fujiwara guardians, who were themselves still riven by family quarrels which led them to neglect public affairs to the extent that the capital itself fell into a state of anarchy and was invested by brigands. The palace was burned down again three more times, but En'yu clung on as titular emperor until his abdication in 984.

65. KAZAN (984–6)

Having been crown prince since infancy, Kazan at the age of 17 was a sensitive youth and promising poet when he succeeded his uncle. Soon after that, his favourite consort Yoshiko died in childbirth, and the grief-stricken young man was cynically persuaded by Fujiwara no Kaneie, his mentor, to seek solace in religion. Pretending, on his father's instructions, that he too was determined to enter the priesthood, Kaneie's son, Michikane, tricked the emperor into going with him by night to the temple of Gango-ji and there abdicating through taking the tonsure. Michikane did not follow suit. Kazan appears to have found a real vocation. He undertook many pilgrimages after his abdication, and developed an interest in political intrigue only during the last years of his life, when he returned to the capital and assumed the title of cloistered emperor. He died at the age of 41.

66. ICHIJŌ (986–1011)

Many years ago the dour Scottish historian James Murdoch in his *History of Japan* dismissed the courtiers of the late Heian period as 'An ever-pullulating brood of greedy, needy, frivolous dilletanti – as often as not foully licentious, utterly effeminate . . . but withal the polished exponents of high breeding and correct "form"'.

The reign of the emperor Ichijo, who was seven when he came to the throne, may be thought of as representing the high peak of refinement in court life, and as justifying in some measure Murdoch's strictures. Three ex-emperors were still alive: Ichijo's father En'yu, his uncle Reizei and his

The Emperor Ichijo

cousin Kazan. Fujiwara Kaneie remained in complete control of court affairs until his own death, which predictably sparked off renewed internecine strife; but a measure of social stability returned when the arrogant but extremely able and effective Michinaga (966–1027) emerged as head of the family.

The divorce of the court nobility from outside reality became total, and though senior nobles nominally had jobs in government, in practice they idled their days and nights away, occupying themselves with various gentle pastimes, poetry, music and tastefully dissolute sexual promiscuity in the company of well-bred court ladies. To the modern reader it appears very dream-like, possibly because few people at court had the slightest interest in the exact time of day or night, or access to a reasonably reliable means of calculating it. It was enough to know that with the coming of first light a gentleman was expected to leave the bed of the lady with whom he had spent the night, make his way to his own quarters through the early dew and compose a 'morning after' poem which convention required him to have delivered to his inamorata without delay.

Life dealt more harshly with those outside the magic circle of privilege. In 988 one of the first recorded acts of *hara-kiri* took place when the outlaw Hakamadare Yasusuke is said to have disembowelled himself to avoid capture alive. The *hara* or abdomen was regarded as the seat of the will, and the source of boldness, anger and generosity in an individual; and suicide after the manner of Yasusuke eventually became ritualised under the more refined name of *seppuku*. Yasusuke himself must have suffered fearfully, since he plunged his sword into himself while standing up and leaning against a pillar, and took more than a day to die.

He was one of the casualties of Michinaga, who ruthlessly restored order in the capital. In Michinaga's time the power of the Fujiwara clan reached its height. He had five daughters, all destined to become imperial consorts. The eldest of them, Akiko, was married to Ichijo in 999 when the emperor was 19 and his bride twelve years old. Cultural activities were the *raison d'être* of court life, with Ichijo himself active as a music lover and man of letters. Akiko, though second in precedence among the court ladies to the empress Sadako, presided over the first identifiable literary salon. Her own ladies-in-waiting included the world's first known novelist, Murasaki Shikubu, author of *The Tale of Genji*. Murasaki's colleague Sei Shonagon's *Pillow Book* is almost equally renowned. It is a commonplace book consisting of short, wry and observant notes on nature, court life and her colleagues, fascinating lists of 'pleasant', 'hateful', 'depressing' or even 'squalid' things (under the last-mentioned she lists the back of a piece of embroidery, the inside of a cat's ear and the seams of a fur robe that has not yet been lined); and acid judgements about the fashion sense of some of her colleagues. Her book must have proved a valuable source of material with which to entertain Akiko, who when bored was apt to summon the wittiest of her attendants at any time of the day or night. A typical entry gives the flavour of her obsessive quest for perfection:

> I cannot stand a woman who wears sleeves of unequal width. If she has several layers of robes, the added weight on one side makes her entire costume lop-sided and most inelegant; if she is dressed in thick

> wadded clothes, the uneven balance prevents them closing properly in front, and this too is very unsightly . . . the smartest robes, after all, are those with evenly matched sleeves that people have worn since ancient times. I don't mind if both the sleeves are very wide, but such robes are rather awkward for Court ladies in ceremonial dress. . . . Fashionable, good-looking people really dress in a most inconvenient way.
>
> (*The Pillow Book of Sei Shonagon*, translated by Ivan Morris, p. 252)

The imperial consort Akiko was clearly a lively-minded woman herself, but in 1026, long after her husband's very early death, she abandoned the artificial world of the court, had her head shaved and became a nun.

67. SANJŌ (1011–16)

Ichijo's successor Sanjo was a son of the retired emperor Reizei, and he became emperor himself in the year of his father's death. A man of 37, he was not so amenable as Michinaga would have wished. He much offended his principal minister when he named a daughter of a less important noble his empress, in preference to one of Michinaga's, and the tension between the two men gradually became such that Sanjo, who suffered from eye trouble, was goaded into abdication after reigning for only four years, dying a year later. The next several emperors were well chosen from the Fujiwara point of view: they were pliable nonentities.

68. GO-ICHIJŌ (1016–36)

The first of these, Go-Ichijo, was nine when he succeeded Sanjo and only 29 when he died, and Michinaga and Yorimichi, his successor as head of the Fujiwara family, had a completely free hand throughout his reign. He left no sons, though one of his two daughters became empress to Go-Sanjo, and he was succeeded by his brother, Go-Suzaku, who was 28 when he became emperor.

69. GO-SUZAKU (1036–45)

Yorimichi retained his powerful position throughout the reign of Go-Suzaku, whose son and successor Go-Reizei likewise made no personal mark. He is reputed to have been a man of intelligence with a scholarly disposition although the Fujiwara allowed him scant opportunity to exercise his talents.

70. GO-REIZEI (1045–68)

His reign was made notable by a serious uprising in the far north. This involved the Abe, a powerful family who claimed imperial descent, and it was not finally suppressed for nine years. Also while he occupied the throne Go-Reizei's palace was on three separate occasions badly damaged by fire.

71. GO-SANJŌ (1068–72)

The brother of Go-Reizei, Go-Sanjo had for that reason been crown prince throughout the previous reign, despite not having had a Fujiwara mother, and he became the first emperor unrelated to the dominant clan since Saga nearly two hundred years earlier. He boldly asserted his independence by relegating his Fujiwara minister Norimichi to the sidelines, and throughout his short reign handled affairs of state personally. His action had dramatic consequences. Once dislodged, the Fujiwara were never to regain their ascendancy over the court.

In order to boost the declining imperial revenues, which no longer attracted Fujiwara subvention, Go-Sanjo revoked some at least of the tax-free land grants sold by his predecessor Saga (52), and the land reverted to the imperial family's ownership. He also forbade the reappointment of provincial governors, whose posts were becoming in effect hereditary. Go-Sanjo abdicated in 1072 in favour of his son, having devised a new, post-Fujiwara system called *Insei*, or government by retired emperors, who would be free to choose their own advisers. Go-Sanjo had intended to be the first to take advantage of it and to continue to govern through his son, but he died soon afterwards.

72. SHIRAKAWA (1072–86)

Coming to the throne at the age of 20 and quickly bereft of his father's advice, Shirakawa kept state affairs in his own hands for the rest of his life. He was a passionately devout patron of Buddhism who enforced his conviction that the taking of animal life was forbidden by ordering the destruction of several thousand fishing nets, which cannot have endeared him to those thus deprived of the means to make a living. He was addicted to elaborate religious ceremonies, and made numerous imperial pilgrimages outside his capital as well as countless formal progresses to temples, some of which he founded, within its bounds. All this cost huge sums of money and the exchequer was soon depleted. Shirakawa then had recourse to precisely the kind of irregular financial practices which his late father had been trying to eradicate. He also allowed himself to be intimidated by the belligerent soldier-monks of the Enryaku-ji temple complex on Mount Hiei, who frequently descended upon the city which their temples had originally been established to protect. Shirakawa abdicated after fourteen years on the throne, yielding it to one of his seven sons (the other six all became priests), but he retained control of the little world of the imperial household through his own court and councils. This arrangement came to be known as cloistered government, lasted about a century and has been aptly described as 'a brilliant holding operation'.

73. HORIKAWA (1086–1107)

Although Horikawa technically reigned for twenty years, he was no more than titular emperor, his father remaining in charge throughout his reign, and continuing to administer the government in the name of his grandson Toba.

74. TOBA (1107–23)

Toba became emperor at the age of five and abdicated when he was only 20. He did, however, come to exercise authority after Shirakawa died in

The Emperor Toba

1129 and he took over the role of cloistered emperor. Toba was an imprudent and extravagant ruler, who lavished favours on his friends, notably members of the military house of Taira, whose rivalry with the Minamoto clan was becoming ever more bitter, and was ultimately to lead to civil war.

CHAPTER FOUR

Child Emperors and Abdications

There had been youthful emperors previously, but the accession of Toba in 1108 marked the beginning of a period of nearly two centuries during which the titular occupants of the throne of Japan were little more than figureheads, prevented by their extreme youth from exercising such limited powers as were still at the disposal of the emperor, and dying or being required to abdicate before reaching maturity. Those who survived long enough after abdication became eligible to join the ranks of the retired or cloistered emperors and their intimates, who schemed and intrigued behind the scenes. Toba (74) had become emperor at the age of five and abdicated at 20 but had a second career of this kind which continued until his death at the age of 54.

75. SUTOKU (1123–41)

His successor Sutoku was also aged five at the time of Toba's abdication, and had to retire twenty years later. But there were no opportunities for him to act as imperial puppet-master, and he died in penurious exile. The short life of the seventy-sixth emperor, Konoe, was likewise unhappy throughout.

76. KONOE (1141–55)

Konoe was a child of three when he was made emperor, and he grew into a shy, sickly youth with very poor eyesight. He died at the age of 17, two years after his plea to be allowed to abdicate was denied by his father, the cloistered former emperor Toba. The latter had other plans, which were, however, upset by Konoe's early death and nullified by his own demise shortly afterwards.

77. GO-SHIRAKAWA (1155–8)

The fourth son of Toba, Go-Shirakawa emerged as emperor after a savage succession dispute – the first since time immemorial to have involved armed struggles between bands of retainers of the leaders of rival court factions – which followed the death of his father in 1156, and which resulted in the exile of his brother, the ex-emperor Sutoku (75). Go-Shirakawa at first sought to be a strong ruler, and when he abdicated after no more than two years as reigning emperor he planned to continue in *de facto* power from the cloister, as Toba had done.

By then, however, the diminished status of the Fujiwara clan in relation to the court had fired the ambitions of the military house of Taira, whose leaders mounted an expedition to investigate the situation in the capital at first hand, with a view to replacing their rivals as guardians of the throne. Taira forces soon occupied Kyoto, and Go-Shirakawa had to face a formidable new opponent in the person of their leader, Taira no Kiyomori (1118–81). Kiyomori had his own connections to the court: he was the brother-in-law of one of the imperial consorts. He was therefore in a position to hear about Go-Shirakawa's plans almost as soon as they were laid, and frustrate them when it suited him to do so. In spite of this, for the rest of his life Go-Shirakawa continued to try to meddle in court affairs, but with only occasional success. He became a Buddhist priest in 1169.

78. NIJŌ (1158–65)

His son Nijo was only 16 when he succeeded, but his youth and inexperience did not prevent his resenting his father's persistent attempts to interfere. In spite of the arrival on the scene of the Taira, senior members of the Fujiwara family remained both politically ambitious and at odds with each other. Some of them close to the young emperor resented the position of their kinsman Michinori, who had the ear of Go-Shirakawa. They therefore sought to bring about his downfall by exploiting the bad feeling between Nijo's court and that presided over by his father; and enlisted the aid of the Taira's rival Minamoto no Yoshitomo in a plot to seize control and bring an end to the parallel system of cloistered government. Choosing a time when Taira no Kiyomori and his principal lieutenants were away from the capital, they assassinated Michinori, placed both the emperor and his father under restraint, and briefly took over the administrative machinery of the imperial court. As soon as Kiyomori became aware of what had transpired he returned to deal with what amounted to a coup d'état. Aided by Taira agents, the emperor escaped from captivity disguised as a maidservant, taking refuge in a safe Taira stronghold. His father too made his escape, and the conspirators, led by Yoshitomo, were overcome.

79. ROKUJŌ (1165–8)

Nijo died and was succeeded by his two-year-old son, while the child's uncle, himself only six, was appointed crown prince. Taira no Kiyomori presided over this convenient arrangement as principal minister (the first non-Fujiwara to rise so high in court status since Sugawara Michizane in the time of the fifty-eighth emperor Koko), and exercised effective power. Kiyomori and Go-Shirakawa for once agreed in wishing to see the crown prince on the throne immediately, and the child Rokujo was deposed by them. Now completely expendable, with no further role at court, the unfortunate lad died when he was thirteen.

80. TAKAKURA (1168–80)

The former crown prince was then elevated to the throne at the age of eight, and came completely under Kiyomori's control. A marriage was arranged when he was eleven with a natural daughter of Kiyomori. The girl had been given imperial status by being adopted by Go-Shirakawa, who had a taste for such scheming, but who nevertheless grew jealous of the influence Kiyomori wielded, and sought anti-Taira allies. Learning of this, in 1179 an exasperated Kiyomori divested Go-Shirakawa of all his formal administrative functions and in effect placed him under house arrest. Kiyomori's action had one unplanned result: it displeased the young emperor Takakura, who abdicated at the age of 20 and died a year later.

81. ANTOKU (1180–3)

The child-emperor Antoku is one of the more celebrated occupants of the throne, because of the manner of his death. He was a casualty of the Gempei war which broke out when leaders of the house of Minamoto (Genji) finally took up arms against the Taira (Heike). Over a period of many years powerful individuals on both sides had sought dynastic and immediate political advantage by marrying their daughters into the imperial family (from which their forebears had originally sprung) and advancing the claims of their favoured candidates for the succession to the throne. Realising that a crisis was imminent, in 1180 Taira no Kiyomori, the veteran chief minister and grandfather of the infant emperor, judged it prudent to move the seat of government away from Kyoto, and went to his own personal estates at Fukuhara in what is now the city of Kobe.

He took with him not only the infant emperor but also the child's predecessor Takakura, and the troublesome but durable Go-Shirakawa. However, the general uproar of protest which this action provoked in the capital obliged even the haughty Kiyomori to change his mind, and after a few months the court was re-established in Kyoto. Kiyomori died in March 1181. His son Munemori attempted to take over the administration, but open civil war was by then raging, and in 1183 Minamoto no Yoshinaka entered and seized the capital. Munemori fled, taking Antoku with him, as well as the widow of Kiyomori and the empress dowager, the boy's mother, who had the sacred regalia in her possession.

The war came to an end in 1185, at the great naval battle of Dannoura on the Inland Sea, which ended in abject defeat for the Taira. In order to avoid capture, Kiyomori's widow, with Antoku in her arms, jumped overboard, and both were drowned. Antoku's mother followed suit with the regalia, but was rescued and the mirror and the jewel were recovered. The sword, said to be the replica made by order of the legendary tenth emperor Sujin, was lost and a replacement had to be made.

The political situation was transformed by the defeat of the Taira, and decisive measures were taken in its aftermath by Yoritomo, head of the victorious Minamoto clan, who was based in Kamakura, some 300 miles to the north-east of the capital. Yoritomo's headquarters there constituted an administrative as well as a military centre. One of its departments (the *samurai-dokoro*) dealt with the administration of the Minamoto vassals, a second (the *kumon-jo*) already handled documents relating to the imperial court, while the third (the *monchu-jo*) was a kind of tribunal which adjudicated on disputes over land rights. This already quite sophisticated organisation was to form the basis of the new, nationwide *and legally constituted* civil government which came formally into existence in 1185 when Yoritomo was commissioned as shogun by the court in the name of the child emperor Go-Toba.

82. GO-TOBA (1183–98)

Yoritomo's appointment was fundamentally unlike those of the generals who had briefly possessed the title in the past. His was for life, and carried with it implied hereditary rights. The shogun's government, to become known as the *bakufu* or camp government, was given plenipotentiary civil authority by the imperial family and the court nobles in return only for guarantees of their revenues and of their privileged social and cultural status. Yoritomo was authorised to assume national police powers by appointing constables (*shugo*) in every province and stewards (*jito*) in every estate. (These titles had Buddhist resonance which also served to underline the legitimacy of the new regime.)

The writings of a contemporary historian, Kujo Ji'en (1155–1225), provide an interesting source of information about the imperial court at this time. He was a Buddhist priest of aristocratic birth, his family, the Kujo, being one of the *Go-Sekke* or five noble branches formed from the extended Fujiwara clan by early in the Kamakura period. The others were called Ichijo, Nijo, Konoe and Takatsukata, and all five remained influential well into the twentieth century. Ji'en was the son of the imperial regent Fujiwara Tadamichi (1094–1164), and his elder brother Kanezane was not only also a regent, but was the man who did most to secure the hereditary title of shogun for Yoritomo in 1185.

Given his background and calling, it is not surprising that Ji'en was chiefly concerned in his work *Gukansho,* which was written in about 1220 when the cloistered emperor Go-Toba and his friends were plotting the overthrow of the Kamakura shogunate, to emphasise the role of Buddhism as 'protector of the state'. To the modern reader, his outlook seems distinctly Machiavellian, no doubt influenced by years of exposure to political in-fighting and intrigue. Indeed, he went so far as to justify the murder of the emperor Sushun (32) in 592 by Soga no Umako as an inescapable religious duty, adding that, in any case, Sushun had been planning to murder Umako.

As might also be expected, Ji'en also defended the historical record of his own Fujiwara clan. His argument, a startling one for a senior Buddhist dignitary to use, was that since they were descended from the deity Ama-no-Koyane, who had been specifically charged by the sun goddess herself to lend a hand to her grandson Ninigi when he descended to earth to pave the way for the first emperor Jimmu, the Fujiwara had as much divine right to 'assist' the throne as the imperial family had to occupy it. Such *parti pris* recourse to Shinto tradition supports the view that the native religion, though eclipsed for several centuries by Buddhism, was still a force to be reckoned with, at least when it provided propaganda ammunition.

Go-Toba had been irregularly installed as emperor in 1184 during the lifetime of the abducted infant emperor Antoku, his brother. The deal was brokered by that indefatigable schemer the cloistered emperor Go-Shirakawa, following complex negotiations between himself and the victorious Minamoto leaders, and was put into effect even though Antoku was, until his death by drowning, in formal possession of the imperial regalia. The meddlesome Go-Shirakawa died in 1192 when Go-Toba was still only twelve years old and barely of an age to understand the sweeping political changes which had further curtailed the influence of the emperor and his court.

An able and versatile youth, he left his mark. He acquired the skills of forging metal so well that he became a swordsmith of some distinction, and was accomplished in the classical arts. Go-Toba was, however, also self-indulgent and extravagant to a degree, and he chafed under the restrictive and essentially meaningless demands of the protocol which his rank entailed. In 1198 at the age of 19 he therefore abdicated in favour of his eldest son, without prior consultation with the shogun, Yoritomo. The shogunal government accepted the *fait accompli*, and Go-Toba was allowed to retain many personal privileges and to cultivate a latent talent for courting disaster.

83. TSUCHIMIKADO (1198–1210)

His successor Tsuchimikado was the oldest of his three sons by three different consorts. He was only four when he became emperor, and 16 when Go-Toba compelled him to abdicate and installed one of his brothers in his place. Tsuchimikado bore his demotion with equanimity: he had not inherited his father's taste for intrigue, and had no liking for the artificial life he had been obliged to live at court. So he submitted a petition to the Kamakura authorities, who allowed him to go to live elsewhere and in modest comfort until his death in 1231.

84. JUNTOKU (1210–21)

His successor Juntoku was Go-Toba's favourite son, and he became emperor at the age of twelve. He abdicated ten years later, in favour of his own infant son, in order to free himself to join his father in the latter's foolhardy plot to encompass the ruin of the shogunate, which was by then dominated by a new political force, the Hojo family.

The balance of power in Kamakura had altered following the death of Yoritomo in 1199. His principal lieutenant, a man of humble origins called Hojo Tokimasa, stepped in and seized effective control of the bakufu administration in typical Japanese style by pulling the strings from behind the scenes. The two sons of Yoritomo duly assumed their father's shogunal title in succession, but both were assassinated, and the post was filled by Minamoto nominees as ciphers who were answerable to Yoritomo's formidable widow Masako. Masako was content to leave the actual shogunal adminstration largely in the hands of Hojo Tokimasa, who was thus left to strengthen further his family's power base in Kamakura.

When Tokimasa died, his son Yoshitoki inherited his administrative role. He further assumed direct executive control of the *samurai-dokoro* or board of retainers, and with it the command of the Kamakura guard and of police authority throughout the city. This may aptly be thought of as the medieval equivalent of seizing the city hall, police headquarters and the radio station. Yoshitoki followed up his bloodless coup by adopting, with the approval of the widow Masako, the title of shogunal regent (*shikken*) or executive deputy. This in classic Japanese fashion became a hereditary post, and the period of Hojo dominance had begun.

Nevertheless, the rise of the Hojos had inevitably been accompanied by a good deal of turbulence in Kamakura, news of which encouraged the former emperor Go-Toba to interfere. He underestimated the strength of Yoshitoki's position and rashly devised a calculated provocation by ordering that certain land-holdings should be transferred to one of his favourite dancing girls. The estates in question had been granted personally by the shogun Yoritomo to Yoshitoki, who was now the undisputed head of the Hojo family. Yoshitoki's response to the insult was to arrange in the name of the shogunal authority for Go-Toba to be formally rebuked. Unabashed, Go-Toba then had the temerity to proclaim Yoshitoki to be an outlaw and his estates confiscated. This astonishing act of defiance outraged not only Yoshitoki himself but also the elder stateswoman Masako, who cherished the memory of her late husband, and it was the catalyst which provoked the so-called Shokyu war. Yoshitoki personally led a punitive expedition towards Kyoto, and easily defeated Go-Toba's small armed force at Uji to the south of the city. Though the reigning emperor Juntoku hastily rescinded his father's rash decree of outlawry, he was banished to the island of Sado, while Go-Toba himself was exiled to the island of Oki. There he spent the last eighteen years of his life in insouciant penury, occupying his time by writing and editing poetry.

Go-Toba's impudent challenge to Kamakura was disastrous not only for Go-Toba himself and for his son Juntoku, but also for those who had been misguided enough to join their cause. Their estates in western Japan were declared forfeit and redistributed among bakufu vassals, temples and shrines. To add to the court's humiliation, Hojo Yoshitoki established a permanent bakufu bureau in the capital, to ensure that no future member of the imperial family overstepped the mark.

85. CHŪKYŌ (1221)

Chukyo is noteworthy on two counts: he reigned, as a child, for only seventy days in 1221 following the abdication of Juntoku, and he was enrolled on the official list of sovereigns and given his posthumous name as late as 1870. The confusion over his status arose because of the brevity of his reign in the aftermath of Go-Toba's ill-starred adventure. Having dealt with the two imperial conspirators, the Hojo forces refused to open negotiations with the guardians of Juntoku's son Chukyo, and promptly ordered his removal from the throne. The lad was treated with consideration, however, being permitted to live comfortably in privileged confinement until his death at the early age of 17.

86. GO-HORIKAWA (1221–32)

At the bakufu's behest, Chukyo was replaced by the ten-year-old son of Go-Toba's elder brother Morisada, who had become a priest but was now, no doubt because he seemed docile, accorded the honours customarily bestowed on a retired emperor. Yoshitoki had no intention of ever again allowing any member of the imperial family a free hand in the capital, and made it clear that without the approval of the two resident Kamakura commissioners in the new bakufu bureau there, neither the young Go-Horikawa nor anybody acting in his name might take any initiative. Go-Horikawa accepted the situation without protest, and his tractability made for the restoration of harmonious relations between the court and the bakufu. When he was 21 the emperor abdicated with the approval of the shogunate in favour of his young son, and died two years later.

87. SHIJŌ (1232–42)

Only four when he became emperor, Shijo is said to have been a very mischievous child. Among other pranks he ordered the wooden corridor floors in the palace to be highly polished so that the ladies-in-waiting might slip and fall down, much to his amusement. Historians relate that unfortunately for him he became a victim of his own practical joke, took a tumble and fell awkwardly, sustaining fatal injuries.

88. GO-SAGA (1242–6)

Of the two obviously eligible candidates to succeed the young emperor Shijo, one was unacceptable to the Hojo because he was the son of the

The Emperor Shijo

exiled Juntoku (84), and if chosen would almost certainly have sought his father's recall to Kyoto. The other was a son of the third living ex-emperor, Tsuchimikado (83). The latter had kept well out of the way during the Shokyu war, and had long demonstrated his lack of interest either in returning to the capital or in political affairs. Go-Saga therefore ascended the throne at the age of 23 and abdicated four years later in favour of his young son, but continued in his long retirement (he died at the age of 49) to exercise the very limited prerogatives now allowed to the throne. Reputed to have been an amiable man with scholarly interests and a retiring disposition, Go-Saga deferred in all political matters to the bakufu, and devoted most of his time to Buddhist studies and observances, making many pilgrimages. This emperor is particularly remembered for the terms of his will. For a very long time it had been generally accepted that the right to nominate the next successor to the imperial throne should, in principle at least, be a perquisite of the senior living former emperor. Primogeniture as such had not been regarded as a question of primary importance, so there was usually a choice of candidates. Go-Saga, however, directed that future emperors should be of the line of his younger son Kameyama rather than that of the elder Go-Fukakusa. Yet in spite of this, at the time of his own abdication he offered Go-Fukakusa a personal sop in the form of a limited spell on the throne.

89. GO-FUKAKUSA (1246–59)

Go-Fukakusa was allowed by his father to reign for twelve years, after which it was understood that he would abdicate in favour of his eleven-year-old brother, who was Go-Saga's favourite son. His retirement, to a temple called the Jimyo-in, formalised the division within the imperial family and the establishment of two rival branches, soon to be generally known as the *Jimyoin-to* or Jimyoin faction and the *Daikakuji-to* or Daikakuji faction. Fraternal love was soon lost between them, and herein lay the origins of the great schism of the fourteenth century.

90. KAMEYAMA (1259–74)

The new young emperor Kameyama was intelligent and precocious, siring the first of his thirty-six children before he was 14. His reign was marked by the first of two armed Mongol incursions into Japanese territory. They were the consequence of a letter sent by Kublai Khan in 1268 demanding tribute from Japan, which went unanswered by either the bakufu or the court of Kameyama. What was interpreted by Kublai Khan as impudent discourtesy led six years later to the mounting of a major expedition, and on 19 November 1274 some 40,000 soldiers landed at Hakata in Kyushu (modern Fukuoka). They were opposed by a much smaller force of Japanese defenders, who fought with valour. The invaders were repulsed, but the decisive factor in their defeat was a storm during the night which scattered the Mongol fleet.

Many enemy soldiers were drowned, but it seems that Kublai Khan did not appreciate the magnitude of his losses, because he despatched an embassy to Japan to renew his demands for submission. His hapless envoys were beheaded on a beach near Kamakura by order of the Hojo regent, who was entirely responsible for foreign policy. Aware that retribution was virtually inevitable, the regent gave orders for the strengthening of the fortifications in Hakata Bay.

There turned out to be plenty of time for this work. During the next five years the Mongols were preoccupied with a campaign in south China, and it was not until 1281 that a new invasion force was sent to Japan. Again the Japanese defenders fought well and held the line for two months before achieving another crushing victory, this time with the aid of an August typhoon which destroyed the invaders' armada. This providential typhoon was dubbed *kamikaze* or divine wind, and the word gained international recognition when it was used towards the end of the Second World War to describe both Japanese one-way bombers and their doomed young pilots.

Kameyama had abdicated in 1274, well before the second Mongol invasion, but remained in effective charge of imperial affairs throughout the thirteen years of the reign of his son Go-Uda. Then in 1289 he entered the priesthood, and until his death in 1305 lived at the Daikaku-ji temple, which had become the headquarters of his branch of the family.

91. GO-UDA (1274–87)

Only seven when his father abdicated in his favour, and himself compelled to abdicate before he was 20, Go-Uda exercised no influence on affairs of state during his reign. He lived on in retirement for many years, but after the death of his principal wife, to whom he had been greatly devoted, he too entered the priesthood.

92. FUSHIMI (1287–98)

Fushimi was the son of the former emperor Go-Fukakusa, who arranged for Fushimi's own son to be appointed crown prince. The nomination outraged Go-Fukakusa's rival the ex-emperor Kameyama of the Daikaku-ji branch, who protested about it to the Kamakura authorities. The regent

Hojo Sadatoki confirmed the appointment of the chosen crown prince, but in doing so laid down new rules. These provided that the succession should thenceforth alternate between the two branches of the imperial family, and that the length of each reign should be no more than ten years. In practice the rule was seldom observed to the letter, but in formally recognising the split the Hojo regent made eventual schism more likely. He also underlined the fact that he regarded emperors as powerless figureheads. Fushimi himself abdicated in 1298, and was influential in strictly family affairs during the reigns of his sons Go-Fushimi and Hanazono.

93. GO-FUSHIMI (1298–1301)

A child of eleven, the crown prince duly succeeded his father, but for only three years. Then, though he had been on excellent terms with the civil authorities in Kamakura, they required him to surrender the throne to a member of the Daikaku-ji branch of the family. He became a priest and retired to the Jimyo-in, where he died.

94. GO-NIJŌ (1301–8)

Go-Nijo became emperor at the age of 17 and died at 23 while still on the throne, the first emperor since the boy Shijo to do so. At the time of his accession there were no fewer than five living ex-emperors, namely Go-Fukakusa, Fushimi and Go-Fushimi of the Jimyo-in branch, and Kameyama and Go-Uda of the Daikaku-ji line. Their survival exacerbated the friction between the two sides of the imperial family, and shows how effective Hojo Sadatoki's ruling was in ensuring that, because of internecine squabbles, there would be no serious imperial challenge to the authority of the shogunate.

95. HANAZONO (1308–18)

Following the death of Go-Nijo, the throne reverted to the Jimyo-in branch, and throughout his reign which began when he was twelve years old,

The Emperor Hanazono

Hanazono did his father Fushimi's bidding. The Daikaku-ji branch formally protested when just over ten years had elapsed, and Hanazono dutifully abdicated to make way for their candidate. During the troubled decades which followed, Hanazono was occasionally in personal danger, but in 1335 he became a priest and lived unmolested thereafter.

Nineteenth-century painting on silk depicting Empress Jingu, in military dress, with General Takeuchi no Sukune and her son the infant Emperor Ojin, fifteenth in the traditional list. Ojin is now believed to have reigned in the late fourth or early fifth century AD.

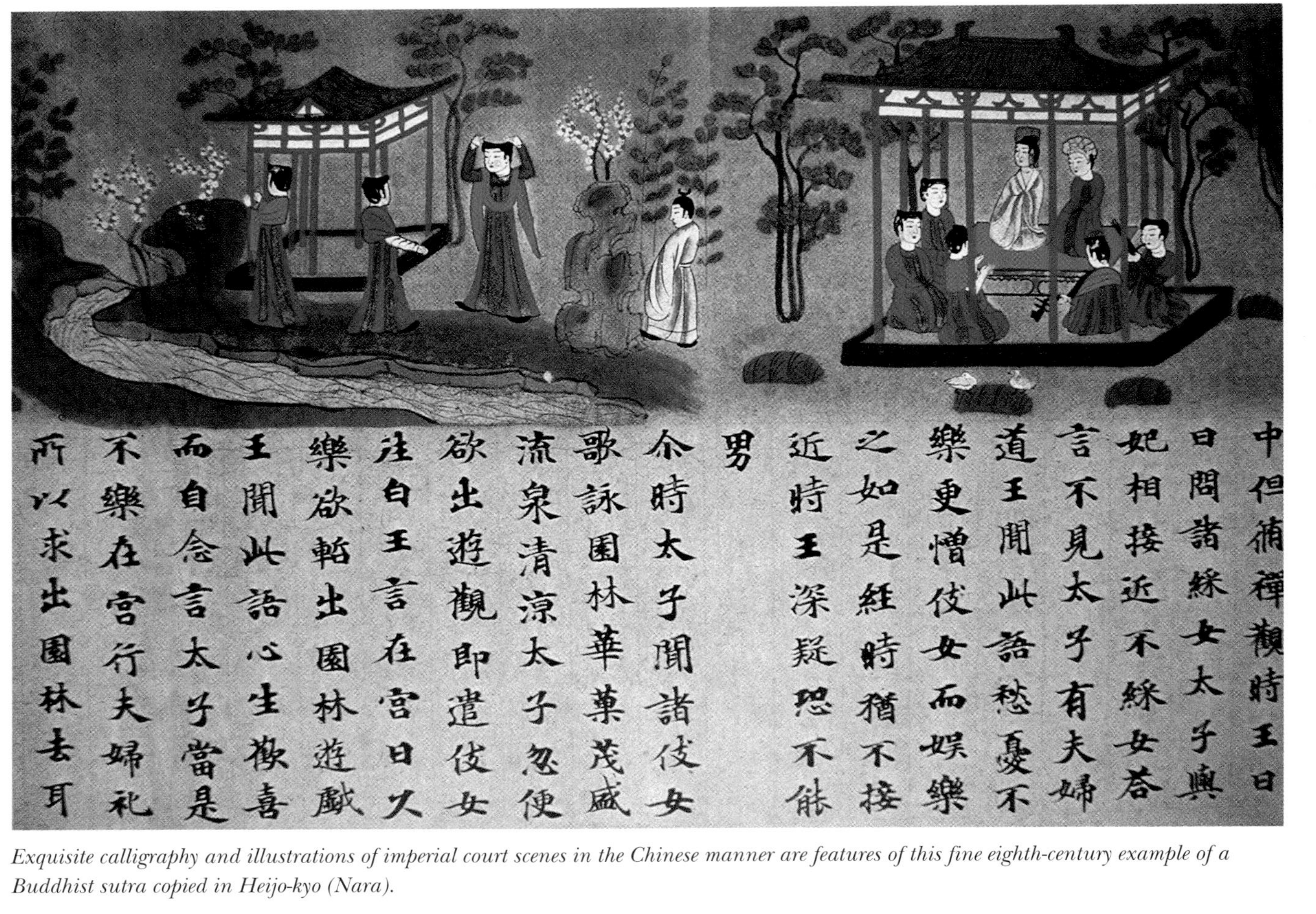

Exquisite calligraphy and illustrations of imperial court scenes in the Chinese manner are features of this fine eighth-century example of a Buddhist sutra copied in Heijo-kyo (Nara).

Part of a narrative scroll, produced in the seventeenth century, giving a romanticised picture of everyday life for the ladies of the imperial court in Heian-kyo (Kyoto), c. AD *1000.*

A seventeenth-century illustration for the enduringly popular Tale of Genji *written by the Heian court lady Murasaki Shikibu,* c. AD *1000. Reckoned to be the earliest example of the novel in world literature, it gives a vivid first-hand picture of life and love in court circles.*

The national hero Nawa Nagatoshi depicted in the presence of Emperor Go-Daigo, to whose cause he rallied when the emperor escaped from exile and briefly regained his throne before the great schism. The nineteenth-century artist has wrongly assumed that Nagatoshi would not have been permitted to see the emperor's person, as was later the case, so only the exterior of his dwelling is shown.

A prince of the Satsuma clan, which was based in Kyushu and was one of the two or three principal agents for the political developments leading to the Meiji Restoration of 1868. The prince is photographed in formal robes, before the abolition of feudalism in 1872. Unchanged for over a thousand years, court dress reveals the Chinese influences of the Nara period.

A Shinto priest photographed in his robes in the early Meiji period (latter half of the nineteenth century). Shinto, embracing elements of the native Japanese religion, Confucianism, and emergent nationalism, was to become an important vehicle for political changes.

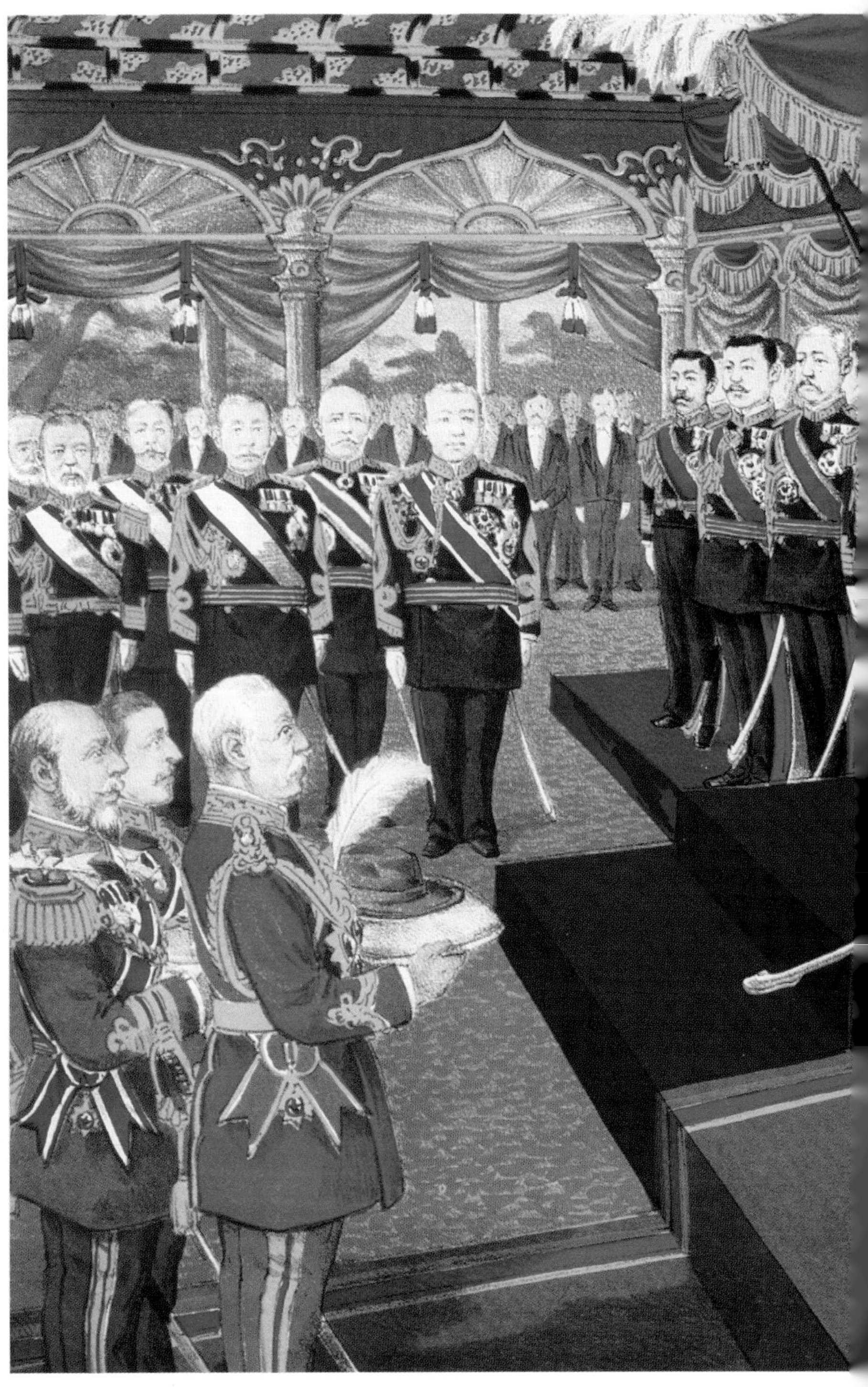

Prince Arthur of Connaught, representing Queen Victoria, investing Emperor Meiji as a Knight of Garter. The British minister and other British and Japanese officials witness the ceremony.

Woodblock print depicting Emperor Meiji with Empress Shoken and Meiji's son Prince Yoshihito (later the emperor Taisho) by Countess Yanagiwara Naruko, one of his official concubines. The impact of Germanic influences, particularly on the new Japanese army, is clear.

CHAPTER FIVE

The Great Imperial Schism

The first chronicles of the history of Japan were followed by a flood of written material, of which a great deal has come down to us. Every important clan built up an archive of records, and most lords ordered the writing of dynastic histories, which were to be consulted for the edification and guidance of generations to come. Literacy as such was slow to spread, but itinerant priests and reciters, often blind, traversed the land and enthralled people of every degree with the entertainment of various kinds they provided. Quasi-history in the form of colourful tales of wars and warriors of the twelfth and thirteenth centuries, composed within living memory of the events they described, gripped audiences for many succeeding generations. Usually compilations of the work of a number of anonymous authors, these epics were much embroidered in the telling, and were especially popular throughout the thirteenth and fourteenth centuries. Five of the so-called 'war tales' survive, of which the *Heike Monogatari*, which deals with the downfall of the house of Taira towards the end of the twelfth century, is the best known, surviving as it does in no less than eighty-eight different versions.

Another is the *Taiheiki*, which tells of the great imperial schism and civil wars of the first half of the fourteenth century. Unlike the *Heike Monogatari*, the *Taiheiki* is believed to be essentially the work of a single scribe, a lowly monk called Kojima of whom little is known. It is far from being great literature, but it does offer a fascinating account of one of the most dramatic reigns in Japanese imperial history: that of the emperor Go-Daigo, who may without too much exaggeration be described as the Bonnie Prince Charlie of Japan.

Go-Daigo's story resembles that of Prince Charles Edward, in that it has elements of romance and a great deal of drama, involving abrupt reversals of fortune, disguises and narrow escapes. Those are not the only respects in which he reminds us of the Scottish pretender, however, for the two men possessed oddly similar personalities as well as being claimants to thrones. Like the ill-starred prince, Go-Daigo was vain, two-faced and cowardly, betraying his own cause and his own most loyal lieutenants. In the process he may well be thought to have engineered the ultimate political extinction of his own branch of the imperial family.

96. GO-DAIGO (1318–39)

In sharp contrast to virtually all his recent predecessors, Go-Daigo was a man of mature years when he succeeded to the throne in 1318. He was, moreover, a politically ambitious one who had been brought up in the atmosphere of longstanding hostility towards the Hojo regents which prevailed in his branch of the imperial family. Unreconciled to the role and status of the shogunate, he had long cherished the ambition to overthrow the supremacy

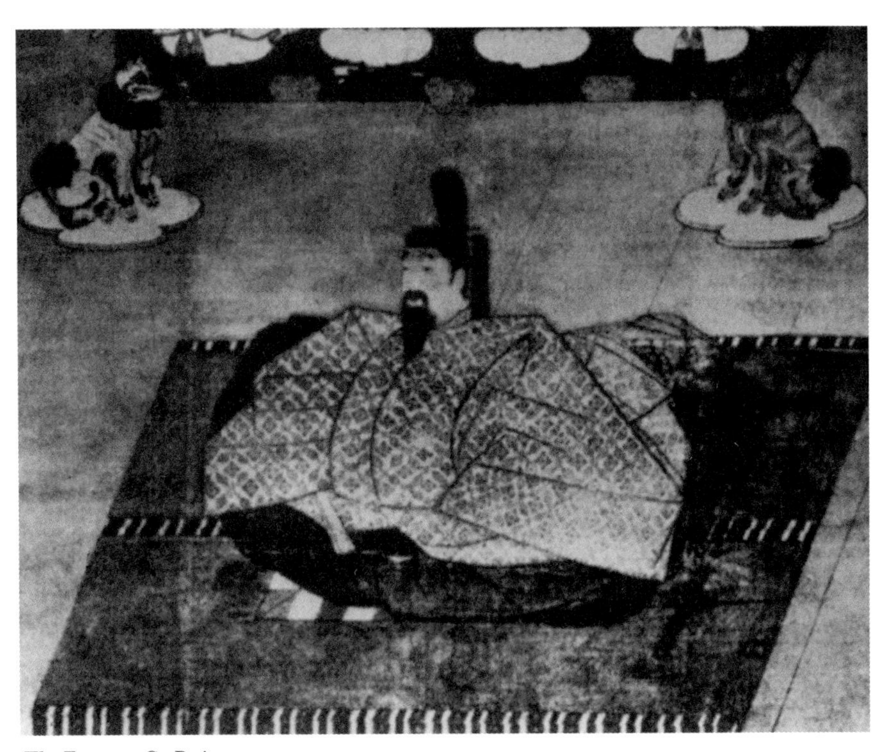

The Emperor Go-Daigo

of the Hojo clan and the whole apparatus of separate civil government, and to restore political power to the throne. Accordingly, soon after he became emperor he embarked on what was in effect a public relations exercise, ostentatiously concerning himself with the welfare of the common people during the great famine of 1321. The new emperor's display of independence, bolstered by the fact that his retired father the emperor Go-Uda had relinquished his residual powers to him, caused alarm in Kamakura. This was so great that when the crown prince (who was of Go-Daigo's own branch) died, the bakufu authorities refused to allow the emperor to appoint his own son to fill the vacancy, insisting that the new heir presumptive should be a son of Go-Fushimi (93) of the amenable Jimyo-in branch.

Nettled, Go-Daigo now embarked on a long, complicated and dangerous course of intrigue, ingratiating himself with the warrior monks of Mount Hiei by despatching two of his sons to live there. He installed one of them as the prince-abbot of the great Enryaku-ji temple complex on the summit of the mountain, and the elder, Prince Morinaga, as chief priest of the Tendai sect to which the Enryaku-ji belonged. By this time Go-Daigo had been on the throne for more than ten years, and should have been astute enough to realise that the rival branch would take no more kindly to his exceeding the time limit than his own close kinsmen had done in the case of the emperor Hanazono. The leaders of the Jimyo-in party were probably not aware of the full extent of Go-Daigo's plotting, but they did press their claim in a formal submission to the bakufu, complaining that the incumbent emperor's retirement was overdue, and adding for good measure that he was not loyal to Kamakura.

The bakufu responded by announcing in September 1331 that a son of Go-Fushimi would become emperor. In a fury Go-Daigo at once denounced the Hojo as rebels, and after commanding that an imperial army should be raised, left the capital by night, taking the regalia with him, and went in secret to Mount Kasagi. He tricked the Hojo by sending his imperial palanquin (with one of his leading supporters inside it) to Mount Hiei, which was duly attacked by Hojo forces. Go-Daigo's two sons renounced their priestly dignities and escaped to join their father, but all three were hunted down and confined at the temple of Byodoin in Uji, south of Kyoto. The Hojo then proclaimed the Jimyo-in prince as the new emperor, and demanded that Go-Daigo should surrender the regalia,

敬白
發願事
右心中所願速疾
令成就者
状如件
元弘二年八月十九日

Written petition by the Emperor Go-Daigo

which had on his instructions been hidden. This he refused to do, whereupon he was taken to the Hojo stronghold in the capital and thence banished to the remote Oki island in the Japan Sea.

Prince Morinaga and his ally Kusunoki Masashige (who are the real heroes of the *Taiheiki*) fought on, remaining in clandestine contact with the exiled emperor by using fishermen as their messengers. Go-Daigo's cause was not lost, because the days of Hojo supremacy were numbered. The last Hojo regent was the disastrously ineffective Takatoki, who died at the age of 30 in 1333. According to the *Taiheiki*, which deliberately set out to blacken his reputation by describing him as a debauchee, 'By day and by night, with wanton acts he dishonoured his glorious ancestors under the ground; in the morning and in the evening, with vain merriment he invited ruin in his lifetime . . . Those who saw knit their eyebrows, and those who heard uttered condemnations.'

The predicted ruin came when the bakufu's senior general Ashikaga Takauji changed sides, and led a force which attacked the Hojo redoubt in Kyoto. This action effectively brought the Kamakura shogunate itself to an end. The leaders of the Hojo clan committed suicide, and in the confusion Go-Daigo contrived to escape from custody and make his way back to the mainland, arriving in Hoki province (now Tottori) where he encountered a loyalist local samurai called Nawa Nagatoshi (d. 1336). Nagatoshi raised forces to support Go-Daigo, and the so-called Kemmu Restoration of the legitimate emperor was accomplished when, without much opposition en route, Nagatoshi escorted him into the capital in triumph in 1333. The temporary imperial replacement, Kogon, was accordingly set aside and compensated by the grant of honours normally accorded to a retired emperor.

Go-Daigo did not handle his reinstatement wisely. He declined to appoint ministers, proposing to govern directly and personally; and though he conferred court appointments on his personal saviour Nawa Nagatoshi (who is still lauded in Japan as an exemplary patriot) he failed to reward the military leaders who had defeated the Hojo and actually engineered his return. In particular he made an enemy of Ashikaga Takauji, to whom he owed so much, and that was the emperor's undoing. Takauji had ambitions of his own, and saw an opportunity to realise them. He took the field again, and after emerging as victor of many skirmishes and some serious battles, in one of which the hero Nawa Nagatoshi was killed, decided that he was in a position to seize the title of shogun for himself. He did so, returning with military support to the capital in 1337. Once securely established there, he nominated a younger brother of Kogon as emperor and demanded that Go-Daigo should surrender the imperial regalia to him.

Go-Daigo deceived Takauji by handing over counterfeits which had been made by his order. It is necessary to distinguish the so-called 'real' regalia from the mirror enshrined at Ise and the sword at the Atsuta Shrine near Nagoya. Replicas of these two items were held by the emperors, with what was allegedly the original jewel, and they gained reverent recognition as the valid, portable emblems of legitimate sovereignty. These Go-Daigo kept in his possession. So the counterfeits surrendered to the new self-appointed shogun were, in the case of the mirror and the sword, in reality copies of replicas.

Having deceived Takauji, Go-Daigo escaped from Kyoto, armed with the 'real' regalia, went south-east with a small band of supporters, and formally initiated what came to be known as the great imperial schism by establishing his own court in a Buddhist temple in the mountain village of Yoshino not far from Nara. There he died.

The schism endured until 1392. For nearly sixty years the northern court in Kyoto, which was now also the seat of the Muromachi (Ashikaga) shogunate, was presided over by sovereigns of the Jimyo-in branch, while emperors of the Daikaku-ji branch reigned over the southern court in Yoshino. The rival sovereigns were all of legitimate imperial blood. However, the 'authentic' regalia being held by the southern emperors, it was they who were eventually accorded official recognition and assigned a place in the traditional list.

97. GO-MURAKAMI (1339–68)

Go-Murakami was a boy of twelve when he succeeded his father in Yoshino, and he reigned there until his death at the age of 40, during a period of perpetual warfare and political turbulence. During these years there were many channels of contact between the two courts, both clandestine and otherwise, and Ashikaga Takauji, uneasy about the legitimacy of his title after discovering that Go-Daigo had successfully deceived him over the regalia, is known to have instigated several unsuccessful attempts to effect a reconciliation. Go-Murakami's court was reinforced by a number of nobles who defected from Kyoto, but this development merely led to the existence of two squabbling factions in Yoshino.

98. CHŌKEI (1368–83)

It was not until 21 October 1926 that Chokei secured formal – albeit belated – recognition as the ninety-eighth emperor of Japan, by authority of a decree of the prince regent Hirohito, himself shortly to become the one hundred and twenty-fourth emperor. This came after many years of dispute among scholars, whose arguments and findings were scrutinised in the 1920s by specialists (equivalent to the heralds of the College of Arms) on the staff of the Imperial Household Ministry. Chokei was the elder brother of Go-Kameyama, and it is now officially asserted that he reigned over the southern court from 1368 to 1383, and died aged 52 in 1394, two years after the end of the great schism.

99. GO-KAMEYAMA (1383–92)

Go-Kameyama is now believed to have acceded to the throne in 1383. Having been in possession of the imperial regalia, he is regarded as the legitimate sovereign throughout his reign, which was marked by a sharp deterioration in the military position of the southern court's forces. A realist, Go-Kameyama in 1392 came to terms with Ouchi Yoshihiro, appointed by the shogun and aesthete Yoshimitsu (1358–1408) to be his chief negotiator. The settlement was sealed when Go-Kameyama proceeded in state to Kyoto, where he was received with extravagant ceremony. By prior agreement, he then promptly abdicated in favour of the incumbent sovereign of the northern court, who was legitimised as the sole and undisputed emperor when Go-Kameyama relinquished the regalia to him. Go-Kameyama lived on in honoured retirement until the age of 78.

The great imperial schism of the fourteenth century has provoked much debate and inspired a great deal of literature over the centuries, beginning with the *Taiheiki.* A curious and presumably final end-note was written in September 1945, soon after General Douglas MacArthur (who came to be known as 'the blue-eyed shogun') had arrived to preside over the Allied occupation of Japan, and the fate of the Showa emperor was very much in question. A letter arrived at MacArthur's headquarters from Kumazawa Kando, a shopkeeper in Nagoya. This advised the general that Kumazawa was the legitimate emperor of Japan, by descent from the Daikaku-ji line. His claim was ignored, as were those of well over a dozen other postwar pretenders to the Chrysanthemum Throne, some of whom may still nourish hopes of better days to come.

To complete the story of the great schism, brief accounts should be given of the northern court sovereigns, who played a significant part in the history of the Chrysanthemum Throne and whose descendants still furnish its occupants. The dates in brackets are those of their births and deaths.

N1. KŌGON (1313–54)

A son of the emperor Go-Fushimi (93), Kogon was first placed on the throne by Ashikaga Takauji in 1331, when the emperor Go-Daigo was dethroned and exiled. He reigned again, this time over the schismatic northern court, following the brief and ill-starred restoration of Go-Daigo before his flight to Yoshino. Kogon died in retirement at a Zen temple in Tamba.

N2. KŌMYŌ (1322–80)

Komyo was Kogon's younger brother, and was elevated by Takauji in 1336. He resigned in favour of his nephew in 1348.

N3. SUKŌ (1334–98)

Komyo's nephew Suko had an eventful career, being captured by forces of the southern court in 1351. Although another candidate immediately took his place, he was confined by them for six years before being permitted to retire to Fushimi, where he died long after the schism had ended.

N4. GO-KŌGON (1338–74)

Following the imprisonment of Suko, Go-Kogon presided over the northern court for twenty years, after which (though still only 34) he gave place to his son.

N5. GO-EN'YU (1359–93)

Go-En'yu followed the example of his father and resigned in favour of his own son, just six years of age, in 1382. The boy was to remain sovereign of the northern court for ten years, and then become the undisputed emperor Go-Komatsu in 1392.

CHAPTER SIX

Hard Times

Just as even the high-ranking Buddhist priest Kujo Ji'en emphasised in about 1220 the continuing importance of Shinto for the Japanese state and the imperial court, so more than a hundred years later did another celebrated historian, Kitabatake Chikafusa (1293–1354), who was a senior courtier and confidential adviser to the emperor Go-Daigo. Chikafusa was personally and bravely involved in the events leading up to the great imperial schism described in the previous chapter, but did not live to witness its end. For him, Shinto was crucial to Japan's uniqueness. When writing his *Jinno Shotoki* or 'Records of the Legitimate Succession of the Divine Sovereigns' he put it very bluntly:

> Great Japan is the divine land. Its foundations were first laid by Kunitokotachi-no-mikoto and it has been ruled since time immemorial by the descendants of Amaterasu Omikami. This is true only of our country; there are no examples among foreign lands. It is for this reason that we call our land the divine land.

By its very nature, Shinto manifested itself primarily in the local worship of countless minor deities. A central national focus did, however, exist, in the form of the two grand shrines at Ise, to the east of Kyoto and not far from modern Nagoya. In one of these, the *Naiku* or inner shrine, the spirit of the sun goddess Amaterasu herself, as represented by the sacred mirror which was the most important of the three items of the imperial regalia, was enshrined; and an imperial princess had long filled the role of resident guardian there. The outer shrine or *Geku* was dedicated to Toyouke, the harvest god. In terms of relative prestige, there was no contest, but each shrine was served by a hereditary priestly family, and the Watarai were responsible for the *Geku*. In a bid to achieve parity of esteem with their rivals, the Arakida who served the inner shrine, and to raise money, the Watarai encouraged pilgrims, who flocked to Ise in great numbers. So-called Ise Shinto, a cult which encouraged reverence for both of the gods enshrined there, promoted new enthusiasm for the sun goddess and for her earthly descendants who occupied the imperial throne. Questions of the succession to the throne therefore had a high priority on the general political as well as the religious agenda. Whoever controlled the incumbent was *ipso facto* in a position of great influence.

100. GO-KOMATSU (1392–1412)

In the case of Go-Komatsu, the strings were pulled by the Ashikaga family. After ten years as the sovereign of the northern court, he was still only 16 when he was recognised as the undisputed and sole legitimate emperor of Japan. His father Go-Kogon, the former northern sovereign, was granted the title of retired emperor, and notwithstanding his enhanced prestige, Go-Komatsu remained the puppet of his original sponsors, such limited prerogatives as remained to the throne being exercised on the young man's behalf by Go-Kogon until his death in the following year.

But the Ashikaga star was waning. In 1397 Yoshimitsu, arguably the greatest shogun of this famous dynasty, handed the title over to his son, becoming instead at his own request the emperor's chief minister – the first member of a military family to hold the office since the days of Taira no Kiyomori. Go-Komatsu himself abdicated in favour of his eleven-year-old son Shoko in 1412, but he outlived the new emperor and continued to administer the affairs of the imperial court for the rest of his life.

101. SHŌKŌ (1412–28)

Shoko's succession greatly angered the still living former southern emperor Go-Kameyama (99), who protested to the shogun that his agreement to the reconciliation settlement of 1392 had been on the understanding that a member of his own branch of the imperial family would succeed Go-Komatsu. This was indeed the case, but Go-Kameyama's claim was ignored. He attempted to rally enough support for an armed challenge, but without success, even though Shoko proved to be a thoroughly unsatisfactory sovereign.

During his sixteen years on the throne (until his death in 1428) he took no interest in family politics, but revealed himself to have a violent, eccentric and unpredictable temperament. In spite of the fact that he was interested in military exercises in general and archery in particular, he professed to be a fervent Buddhist and a vegetarian. He was also a quarrelsome drunkard, who frequently beat the helpless palace women about the back with the flat of his sword. He was the father of three daughters, but later, becoming obsessed with Tantric magic, he abstained from sex in the belief that continence would enhance his powers. It did little to prolong his life, however, for he died while still under 30.

102. GO-HANAZONO (1428–64)

Before Shoko's death, his father Go-Komatsu had urged him to adopt Prince Sadafusa, the grandson of the third northern sovereign Suko, and make him his heir. But Shoko flew into one of his violent rages and could not be persuaded to comply. Sadafusa, perhaps prudently, left the capital and became a Buddhist priest, and Go-Komatsu adopted his ten-year-old son instead. The boy duly succeeded Shoko and became the emperor Go-Hanazono, presiding over an impoverished court for thirty-six years.

Hard times for the court reflected the state of the nation as a whole. In 1441 the shogun Ashikaga Yoshinori was assassinated, and with his death even the semblance of central government collapsed. The writ of the shogunate ran only in the region of the capital itself: the rest of the country was the preserve of contending provincial warlords. Yet even in this perilous situation dynastic intrigues continued to be a feature of life at court, and Go-Hanazono's reign was characterised by a succession of plots on the part of the southern Daikaku-ji branch to exploit the general descent into lawlessness and regain the throne.

One of these led, in 1443, to an attempt to abduct Go-Hanazono from the palace itself, which was set on fire. The emperor escaped, but the conspirators seized the regalia, and took refuge in the Mount Hiei temple complex. There they were attacked and defeated by forces of the lame-

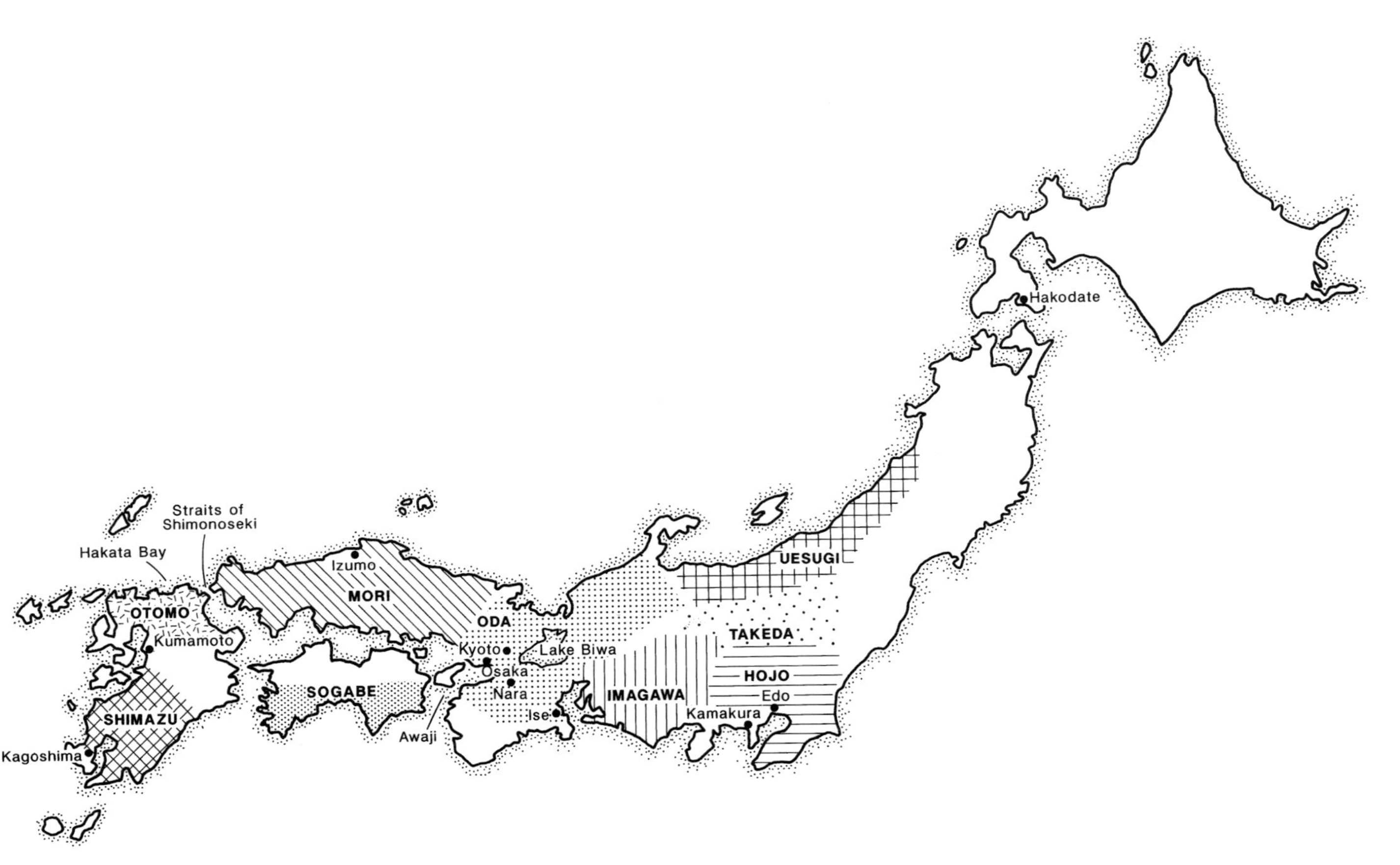

Clan spheres of influence, c. 1500

duck shogunate, which was still in a position to mount small-scale local military operations, and two of their leaders were obliged to commit *seppuku.* Their followers made off in disorder, dropping the sword, which was retrieved and restored to the custody of the court. The rebels did, however, escape in possession of the jewel, and by virtue of this imperial token tried unsuccessfully to re-establish a southern court at Yoshino. After many abortive attempts to recover it, the jewel was finally returned to Kyoto in 1458. Go-Hanazono abdicated in 1464 and was succeeded by his son.

103. GO-TSUCHIMIKADO (1464–1500)

Like his father, Go-Tsuchimikado reigned for well over thirty years, but he inherited an increasingly chaotic realm. The Onin Wars of 1467–77 were one chapter in a century-long story of anarchy and power struggles among provincial warlords, but that particular conflict saw the almost literal destruction of Kyoto, so that it is something of a surprise – and perhaps evidence of the reverence for the throne revived by Ise Shinto – that the imperial institution survived. For more than a decade Kyoto was a battleground fought over by the armies of the Yamana and the Hosokawa clans, and when the imperial palace was itself set ablaze, the emperor and his father were persuaded to take refuge in the shogun Yoshimasa's redoubt in the Muromachi district to the south-west of the palace.

This was one of the few significant buildings still standing in the capital, and there Go-Tsuchimikado remained confined, helpless and divorced from the political situation for thirteen long years, while the city was ravaged. All court ceremonies and ritual celebrations were held in abeyance during that time. Even after the troops were finally withdrawn in 1477 and new quarters were provided for the emperor and his attendants, the replacement 'palace' was a poor and shabby building with only a bamboo fence to protect it. The imperial estates had been laid waste by war, and revenues from them had dried up so completely that after Go-Tsuchimikado died in 1500 his funeral had to be delayed for forty-four days for want of funds to pay for it. Eventually a private donor called Sasaki Takayori provided the money as an act of devotion to the throne, and the remains of the late emperor were interred at Senyu-ji temple.

104. GO-KASHIWABARA (1500–26)

Shortage of funds was also the reason why Go-Tsuchimikado had not, though he wished to do so, abdicated before he died. The abdication procedure involved among other ceremonies a formal visit to Ise by an imperial messenger with an extensive retinue, his function being to 'report' the abdication before the shrine of the sun goddess. Revenues were simply not available to meet the cost of the journey or all the elaborate rituals at Ise.

The new emperor soon realised that abdication was not an option for him either. Indeed only the first, relatively straightforward but essential rituals of his accession were carried out; these consisted of a formal announcement before the replica of the sacred mirror enshrined within the imperial palace itself, and the acceptance by the new emperor of custody of the sword and the jewel. Go-Kashiwabara had to wait twenty-two years for the complicated and long-drawn-out second and third stages, which the shogun Yoshitane eventually funded from his own resources in order to provide the underpinnings of legitimacy, and reinforce the emperor's sacerdotal functions. Go-Kashiwabara died four years later, having known nothing but civil war throughout his lifetime.

105. GO-NARA (1526–57)

The shogunate was able to afford only the simplest of funerals for Go-Kashiwabara, and like him, Go-Nara had to wait for many years until the second and third stages of his coronation could be paid for. The finances of the imperial house itself were exiguous in the extreme, the palace was a virtual ruin, and the new emperor, a learned, scholarly man, was obliged to earn his own living. This he did with his writing brush, by selling his autograph, and by writing and copying poems on commission for those parvenu provincial notables who were relatively well off and considered it chic to possess and display a specimen of the imperial calligraphy. It is recorded that, having formally requested in advance an audience with the emperor, the Jesuit missionary Francis Xavier arrived in Kyoto in 1551. He was unprepared for what awaited him. His first sight of the devastated city horrified him, and when he was made aware of the desperately reduced personal circumstances of an emperor stripped of all political power and influence, he left again without seeing Go-Nara.

106. ŌGIMACHI (1557–86)

Go-Nara's son and successor Ogimachi was 40 years old when he came to the throne, and the imperial finances were still in a parlous state. After a delay of three years, however, a private benefactor paid for the coronation rituals to be completed. Following a century of turbulence throughout Japan, the so-called age of the warring states was drawing to an end. Three men were the architects of a new era. The first of these was the ruthless warlord Oda Nobunaga, who proved more ambitious and effective than his neighbours; he gradually gained personal hegemony over a wide area from his power base in Owari in central Japan.

Remembering that his father Go-Nara had, during one particularly desperate period, successfully appealed to Nobunaga for modest financial help, Ogimachi in 1562 sent him a message begging him to come and pacify the capital. There was no response, and it was not until six years later that Nobunaga had become strong enough to act upon a renewed plea for help from Ogimachi. Then he marched on Kyoto accompanied by Yoshiaki, the last of the Ashikaga shoguns, and entered the city on 9 November 1568. He quickly imposed civic order, provided funds to meet the cost of the construction of a new palace, and, with new grants of land confiscated from the opponents he had defeated, restored the imperial revenues to a much sounder level. Though content to remain in theory the deputy of the shogun, in 1573 Nobunaga imprisoned Yoshiaki following a quarrel between the two men. Yoshiaki nevertheless lived on for another thirty years.

During Ogimachi's reign Christian missionaries more persevering than Francis Xavier made some headway in a number of fiefdoms (from one of which envoys were despatched to Rome) and even in Kyoto itself. Much displeased, Ogimachi twice issued edicts forbidding the propagation of the alien religion, but Nobunaga, though no friend of the Buddhist establishment, neither endorsed nor attempted to enforce them.

In 1582 Nobunaga was assassinated, but his efforts to reunite the country were carried on with considerable success by a military genius of plebeian origins, Toyotomi Hideyoshi, who was based in Osaka. Hideyoshi was effusively respectful to the throne, but in spite of his great wealth and vulgarly extravagant lifestyle, he proved rather less open-handed towards the emperor than Nobunaga had been. So the imperial family's lifestyle remained in sharp contrast to that of the dominant warlords: a contrast so obvious that it was noted by an astute English observer at the time of Elizabeth I, whose name unfortunately is not recorded, nor that of his informants:

> . . . all the wealthe and substance of Japonia, as well private as publicke, dependeth of a fewe, and those fewe of one [Tokugawa Ieyasu] who is lorde of Tenza, whoe without any stay or lette, gyveth and taketh away whatsoever he will . . . This form of regiment causeth continuall revolutions and changes of the states: fyrste because that Dairis [the emperor] (whoe, although hee neither hath power nor empire, yet is held in great estimation and honour with the people) is the cause that the lordes of Tenza and other princes are accounted tyrantes, vsurpers, destroyers of the monarchye, and enemies of the greatnes of Japonia; which thinge taketh away their estimation, and hindreth them of the good will of the people. Hereof it cometh that they are easily moved to take armes . . .
>
> (Quoted in Rundall, *Memorials of the Empire of Japon*, p. 10)

In 1586 Ogimachi's son and heir presumptive died. Nevertheless, the emperor abdicated some months later, in favour of his 16-year-old grandson.

107. GO-YŌZEI (1586–1611)

The imperial fortunes began to improve, in a material if not a political sense, after the accession of Go-Yozei. His reign was given an auspicious start, because Hideyoshi had decided to take up residence in the capital, and had a splendid palace built for himself in Kyoto. It was completed in

The Emperor Go-Yozei

1587, and Hideyoshi invited the young emperor and his grandfather to visit him there on the following New Year's Day. They accepted, and were lavishly entertained for five days; it was the first public appearance by an emperor for well over sixty years.

Unlike his predecessor Nobunaga, the parvenu Hideyoshi aspired to establish a line in his own name, and set scholars to work to fabricate a genealogy purporting to prove his descent from the Fujiwara. He made some progress in his lifetime, accumulating as many resounding court titles as Nobunaga and gaining imperial permission to nominate his adopted son to succeed him in his court offices, but these dynastic plans foundered after his death in 1598. His only serious rival, Tokugawa Ieyasu, seized his opportunity, and Hideyoshi's leaderless followers were defeated by Ieyasu's army at the decisive battle of Sekigahara. Go-Yozei rode the wave by investing Ieyasu as his new hereditary shogun, tactfully accepting Ieyasu's fraudulent claim to be of Minamoto blood.

Ieyasu did not elect to base himself in Kyoto, and, once he had achieved legitimate authority through Go-Yozei, made no further attempt to ingratiate himself personally with the emperor in the way that both Nobunaga and Hideyoshi had done. He established his headquarters in Edo (Tokyo) in 1603, and emphasised the long-term nature of his plans by building a great moated castle there. The imperial seal of approval of Ieyasu's clear-cut victory ushered in the longest period of peaceful national stability in Japan's history, not to mention final acceptance by the court of its decidedly subordinate status. Go-Yozei thereafter did his appointee's bidding, even referring to the shogun a dispute over which of his own sons should succeed him, and accepting Ieyasu's ruling, which was not in fact to the emperor's liking. Ieyasu saw political advantage in ostensible deference to the throne, but in the matter of the imperial finances was hardly more generous than Hideyoshi. However, the new bakufu did assume responsibility for keeping the imperial palace in good repair. As the years went by, Go-Yozei developed a little too much independence of spirit for the bakufu to accept, and in 1611 he was effectively required to abdicate, living thereafter in retirement.

108. GO-MIZUNOO (1611–29)

One of the authentically longest-lived of the emperors, Go-Mizunoo came to the throne as a youth of 16. He showed much early ability as a scholar, and became a devout Zen Buddhist. He was possessed of a mind of his own and a strong will which before long brought him into conflict with the man who had chosen him to succeed his father. Ieyasu wanted to forge a Fujiwara-style relationship with the imperial house by arranging a marriage between his daughter and Go-Mizunoo, who, with the support of the retired emperor Go-Yozei, resisted the idea for a very long time. It was indeed not until 1620, after Ieyasu's death and that of Go-Yozei, and following an open dispute with Ieyasu's son and successor Hidetada, that Tokugawa Kazuko was finally married to Go-Mizunoo with extravagant pomp.

This only served to emphasise the contempt in which the emperors were now held by those who had grasped political power. As our Elizabethan commentator put it:

> In tyme, encreased ambition, and they advancynge and exalting themselves, one while the one, and another while the other, became lordes, he of one parte, and the other of another parte of the empire; taking vppon them the title of Jacatai, that is, of Kynges. Notwithstandynge, they lefte to Dairis the name of Universall Lorde of Japonia, but without either iurisdiction or seignorie. These princes, who have gotten the dominions that are neere to Meacum [Kyoto], scarcelye aforde him meate and aparell, insomuch that there remayneth to him, of auncyente greatnesse and monarchy of Japonia, nothing almost, but, as it were, a shadowe thereof.
>
> (Rundall, op.cit., p. 9)

The hard realities were all too literally brought home when, in 1626, Hidetada and his son Iemitsu made a formal visit to Kyoto and proceeded to humiliate the emperor by requiring him, accompanied by his Tokugawa consort, to call on them at Nijo Castle, the opulent shogunal residence in Kyoto. After enduring a succession of petty procedural insults designed to underline his impotence and to break his will, the worm eventually turned in 1629. None of his sons having survived, Go-Mizunoo, without reference to Edo, abdicated in favour of his seven-year-old daughter. Granted only a minimal stipend – which was, it must be said, considerably enhanced in 1643 – Go-Mizunoo lived until his death at the age of 84 at Shugakuin in the northern suburbs of Kyoto, on a small estate which is still designated as an imperial palace.

109. MEISHŌ* (1629–43)

The little girl Meisho was the penultimate empress regnant, and because of her Toklugawa blood the bakufu met the enormous cost of her coronation rituals, at which many of the old ceremonies which had fallen into disuse during the great north–south schism were revived. Her father supervised

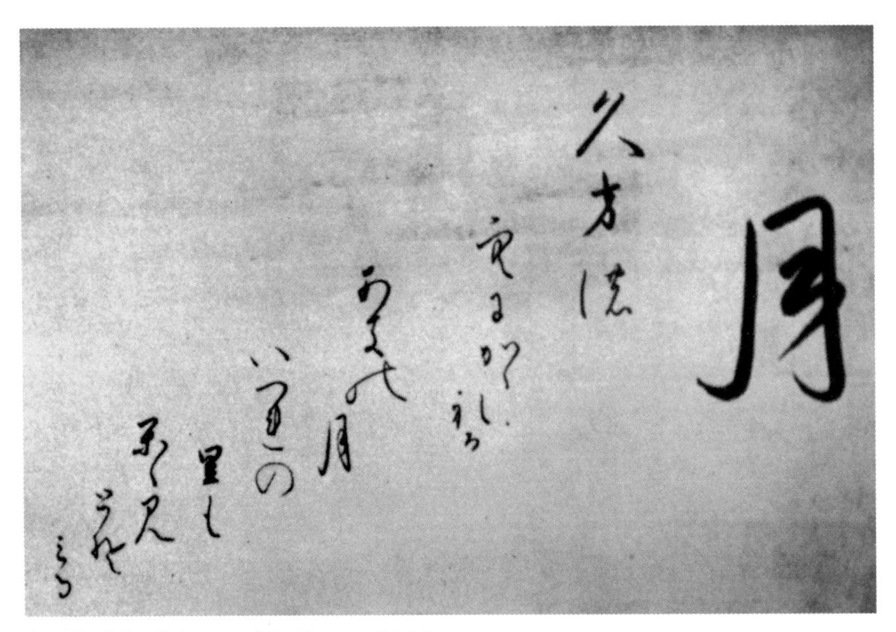

A waka (31-syllable poem) by Empress Meisho

the empress during her childhood, and arranged, with bakufu approval, for her to cede the throne to her half-brother the crown prince when she was still not yet 20. Meisho never married, probably because the existence of a spouse and possible children would have posed serious protocol problems, and might well have threatened a return to the interminable succession disputes of past years; but she lived on in comfort to the age of 74.

110. GO-KŌMYŌ (1643–54)

Becoming emperor at the age of ten, Go-Komyo was a studious and earnest child, a sinologue who rejected native Japanese literature and instead immersed himself in Confucian political theory at a time when Buddhism was still regarded in political circles as the best guide to the arts of government. His fondness for military exercises coupled with various indications that he nourished the idea of ruling as well as reigning alarmed the bakufu, to the extent that Go-Komyo's death at the early age of 21 raised suspicion in many quarters that he had been poisoned on instructions from Edo. The less interesting explanation is that he died of chickenpox. This is more likely, since the succession had yet to be clearly decided.

111. GOSAI (1654–63)

Gosai was a half-brother of his predecessor, and was nominated by the retired emperor Go-Mizunoo. Since the late Go-Komyo left a daughter but no son, and the bakufu did not wish to see another woman on the throne it had been necessary to widen the search outside the narrow confines of the imperial household. He was not an obvious choice, because he had been adopted to head a cadet branch of the imperial family, the Arisugawa, and had to be restored to the purple to succeed to the throne. Although Gosai was only 18 at the time, the unfortunate young man was blamed for a series of disasters which occurred during the ensuing five years. These included two devastating fires in Edo, the seat of civil government, in 1657 and 1658. They were shortly followed by the destruction of the imperial palace in Kyoto by fire. Even more ominously, one of the two grand shrines at Ise burned down in 1661; and when major earthquakes resulted in much damage in various parts of the country in the following year, elements within the Edo government themselves found a convenient Confucian explanation in the theory that the emperor was *ex officio* the chief mediator between heaven and earth, and passed the buck by attributing such a catalogue of disasters to moral shortcomings, or more precisely a lack of virtue in the current incumbent of the throne. Accordingly Gosai was effectively deposed, being compelled to abdicate in 1663, and, though he had eleven sons and seventeen daughters, they were thought insufficiently 'virtuous' to be considered eligible. Go-Mizunoo therefore nominated another half-brother in preference to any of them. Though granted the titles and precedence due to a former emperor, Gosai spent the rest of his life in secluded disfavour.

CHAPTER SEVEN

Improving Fortunes

The Tokugawa shogunate not only survived its first few decades; by the latter half of the seventeenth century it was already showing its potential durability. Moreover, it could already be thought of with rather more accuracy as 'the Edo bakufu'. For though the shogunal title continued to pass by inheritance to members of the Tokugawa family, few of Ieyasu's descendants with the exception of his grandson Iemitsu were endowed with even a modicum of his political genius. That being the case, their court came within a few decades to resemble in many respects that of the imperial family in Kyoto. Just as the emperor was in effect little more than a privileged prisoner, confined to his palace and its immediate vicinity, comprising a total area no bigger than a modern football stadium, so the shoguns came to exercise merely ceremonial, token authority in the inner apartments of the huge castle in Edo. The civil government of the nation was in the hands of their 'advisers'.

On the whole, these statesmen were efficient administrators, albeit with limited horizons. It was Ieyasu's grandson Iemitsu who had ordered the expulsion of all foreigners in the 1630s. By so doing, Iemitsu initiated the policy of seclusion which reduced foreign trade to the merest trickle, through a single Dutch depot on the tiny man-made island of Deshima in Nagasaki harbour, which just two trading vessels were permitted to enter in the course of each year. That policy was to endure in the hands of his political successors at the head of the Edo bakufu for two hundred years. With continued peace came prosperity and, for the imperial house in Kyoto, increasing pomp.

112. REIGEN (1663–87)

Reigen was a boy of ten when he became emperor, and his father the retired emperor Go-Mizunoo administered imperial affairs on his behalf

Reigen as cloistered emperor

for the next fourteen years, until his own death, by which time the young emperor had acquired consorts. Among these was a noblewoman from the influential Takatsukata branch of the original Fujiwara clan, who was the mother of Reigen's fourth son. At the instance of the bakufu this prince was promoted over the heads of his elder brothers and named as heir apparent in 1682. His advancement disappointed Reigen, who would greatly have preferred his favourite son, the eldest, who had, however, been born of a concubine of lesser rank.

To mark the occasion, the bakufu revived the full ceremonial ritual for the investiture of a crown prince, which had been in abeyance for over three hundred years. Perhaps by way of consolation, Reigen was pensioned off liberally when he abdicated five years later, and was treated by the Edo authorities to a grand formal pilgrimage to Kumano at their expense. In active retirement Reigen lived to a ripe old age, administering the minimal business still discharged by the court throughout the next reign.

113. HIGASHIYAMA (1687–1709)

Though he occupied the throne for twenty-two years, Higashiyama had little say in the affairs of the imperial family, invariably deferring to his father for the whole of that period. This saw a considerable improvement in the financial position of the imperial family, and also the regeneration of the capital city. Once a year the head of the Dutch 'factory' in Nagasaki was obliged to make a journey to Edo to pay his respects (and offer costly gifts) to the shogun. The physician and versatile scholar Engelbert Kaempfer was a member of his suite in 1691, and when he passed through Kyoto he found much to please the eye and impress him.

> . . . the women were all on this occasion richly apparell'd in variously colour'd gowns, according to the fashion of Miaco [Kyoto], wearing a purple color'd silk about the forehead, and large straw-hats to defend themselves from the heat of the sun. We likewise met some particular sorts of beggars, comically clad, and some mask'd in a very ridiculous manner [these were probably medicant Zen monks], not a few walk'd upon iron stilts; some were singing, some whistling, some fluting, others beating of bells . . . There is scarce a house in this large capital, where there is not something made or sold. Here they refine copper, coin money, print books, weave the richest stuffs with gold and silver flowers. The best and scarcest dyes, the most artful carvings, all sorts of musical instruments, pictures, japan'd cabinets, all sorts of things wrought in gold and other metals . . . are made here in the utmost perfection.
>
> (*Kaempfer's History of Japan*, vol. III, p. 16)

Following the revival of the formal ceremony for the investiture of a crown prince sponsored by the bakufu in Reigen's time, other court rituals, long fallen into disuse or at best perfunctorily observed in abbreviated token form, were researched and reinstated. The continuing popularity of Ise Shinto had done much to stimulate general interest, and that of scholars and antiquarians in particular, in the indigenous religious roots of the imperial institution and the sacerdotal and mystical role of the emperors. This in turn promoted scholarly research into the historical development of the secular monarchy as influenced by Chinese and Confucian models. With the approval of the authorities in Edo, attention was turned specifically to the rituals prescribed in ancient times for the coronation of a new emperor.

These consisted, and still consist, of two discrete, protracted sequences of observances, which were revived in all their former leisurely dignity for the emperor Higashiyama. The first sequence involves very elaborate processions, formal announcements and offerings before various shrines, and is known as the *sokui-rei,* or 'ascending the throne'. The second is the esoteric *Daijosai,* or Great Thanksgiving ceremony, always conducted in November, and no more than once in each reign. Its climax is a symbolic and mystical act of communion between the sun goddess Amaterasu and the emperor, during which he consumes new rice which has been grown with great and reverent ritual specially for the ceremony. Each of these series of rites take a year or more to carry out. It is fortunate therefore that to some extent they can be conducted in parallel. The emperor Higashiyama acted as something of a guinea pig during the reconstruction of these long-neglected ceremonies, and throughout his reign he was cosseted. Although his occupation of the throne was also marked by a thoroughly inauspicious eruption of Mount Fuji (the last on record), the emperor was, happily, not charged by Confucians in Edo with responsibility for it. Indeed, the bakufu did still more to demonstrate respect for the throne from which it derived its legitimacy, by arranging for the proper identification of and repairs to many of the imperial mausolea, dilapidated after centuries of neglect. Higashiyama abdicated in 1709 in favour of his eight-year-old son, and died only six months later.

114. NAKAMIKADO (1709–35)

Reigen once more acted as regent, this time for his grandson, the new emperor Nakamikado. After the old man's death Nakamikado, by then over 30, finally took charge of court affairs himself, but ruled only for another five years up to his abdication in 1735. The most significant event during his reign, because it was destined to have an important bearing on the future of the imperial house, was the presentation to the bakufu in

1720 of a massive new chronicle, the *Dainihonshi*, or Great History of Japan. This monumental work of scholarship had been compiled on the instructions of Tokugawa Mitsukuni, lord of Mito, who in spite of his illustrious name and family connections with the shogunate was persuaded that the powers of the shogun should properly reside with the throne. Through his initiative in making up-to-date historical research more widely available (in partial manuscript form: it was not printed and published in full as a book until 1906), he helped to pave the way for the ultimate collapse of the Edo government and the consequent restoration of the imperial house to political prominence. Nakamikado abdicated in 1735, dying two years later at the age of 37. He was succeeded by Sakuramachi.

115. SAKURAMACHI (1735–47)

Three years after his accession he also underwent the full coronation ceremonies, including the *Daijosai* rite. His twelve years on the throne were unremarkable, and Sakuramachi is chiefly remembered as the father of the last female sovereign of Japan.

116. MOMOZONO (1747–62)

Though he reigned for fifteen years, Sakuramachi's successor Momozono died soon after reaching manhood. His tenancy of the throne was nevertheless noteworthy in that he came under the influence of nobles in his entourage who, stimulated by the newly available Great History of Japan, were attracted by the work of intellectuals who sought a synthesis of Confucian doctrines with Shinto, itself still a fashionable subject of earnest philosophical discussion. One of these courtiers, Ogimachi Sanjo Kintsumu, became fired with the idea of a future imperial restoration, and induced the young emperor to study the old histories of gods and emperors, giving him many lectures on the subject. His activities came to the notice of the bakufu, who put a stop to them by arresting and punishing Kintsumu and his associates. Nevertheless it was during Momozono's reign that the first political moves towards the historic upheaval of the Meiji restoration were made.

117. GO-SAKURAMACHI *(1762–70)

Momozono left two sons, but the elder of them was only four, and it was decided by the Edo government that until he grew up one of his aunts, a daughter of the emperor Sakuramachi, should occupy the throne. Go-Sakuramachi was 23 when she became empress regnant. Unless the law is again changed, she was and will be the last woman to occupy the imperial throne. For under the provisions of the Imperial Household Law of 1889, only males were thenceforward eligible to succeed; a rule which might just possibly have to be revoked in the future since neither of the present emperor's sons has male issue. Like her predecessor the empress regnant Meisho, and probably for the same reason, Go-Sakuramachi never married, although she also lived in retirement for many years. However, she remained empress for only eight years before handing over as arranged to her nephew, once he reached adolescence.

118. GO-MOMOZONO (1770–9)

Go-Momozono was another emperor who died inconveniently young, at the age of 22, leaving only an infant daughter. His premature death made it necessary to convene a formal council to appoint a successor. The retired empress was consulted for form's sake, but the candidate she favoured was not acceptable to the bakufu, who chose instead a ten-year-old great-grandson of the emperor Higashiyama. His father was Prince Kan'in, head of a cadet branch of the imperial family, and as emperor the boy came to be known as Kokaku.

119. KŌKAKU (1779–1817)

During his minority, Kokaku was in no position to annoy the Edo authorities, and good relations between the shogunate and the imperial court continued for many years. After a great fire which razed much of Kyoto including the imperial palace, the bakufu paid for the construction of new, much grander premises which were sufficiently spacious to permit the staging of the most elaborate of the old court ceremonies as researched and reconstructed by scholars. The emperor and the retired empress Go-Sakuramachi moved into the magnificent new palace in 1790.

This must have been greatly to the satisfaction of the celebrated eccentric Takakura Hikokuro (1747–93), whose reverence for the nobility and the imperial line led him to make many pilgrimages to Kyoto. Here he performed ostentatious acts of devotion such as prostrating himself on Sanjo Bridge with his head in the direction of the imperial palace, and of extravagant loyalty as when he publicly whipped the grave of the long-dead shogun Ashikaga Takeuchi. Takakura's tireless proclamation of the sole legitimacy of imperial authority so irritated the bakufu that after some time he was banned from Kyoto. Thence he went to Kyushu to try to stir up enthusiasm for his brand of loyalism there, but he was pursued by agents of the shogunate, and eventually committed suicide. The prospect of a mass movement in support of the throne clearly made the authorities in Edo extremely nervous. Whether or not the emperor Kokaku ever personally knew that he had such an infatuated subject, he was in many ways worthy of respect, being an able scholar, and scrupulous in the performance of his ritual duties.

His cordial relationship with the Edo authorities came to an end, however. Disliking the fact that his ministers of state took precedence over his own father Prince Kan'in Sukehito, the emperor proposed to bestow on the prince the honours given to ex-emperors. This was in no way an improper or even unusual step; but for reasons which are not clear Matsudaira Sadanobu, the shogun Ienari's chief adviser, put obstacles in the emperor's way, and finally flatly defied an imperial command. Kokaku's father died in 1792 and his proposal was consequently shelved. (The imperial court's collective memory is long, however, and almost a century later, in 1884, Sukehito was posthumously granted the status which had been sought for him in his lifetime by his son.) Kokaku, who was the first emperor for a hundred years to savour the freedom to travel about his capital and enjoy its sights, reigned for thirty-six years before retiring in favour of his own son. He continued to be active in imperial affairs virtually up to the time of his death.

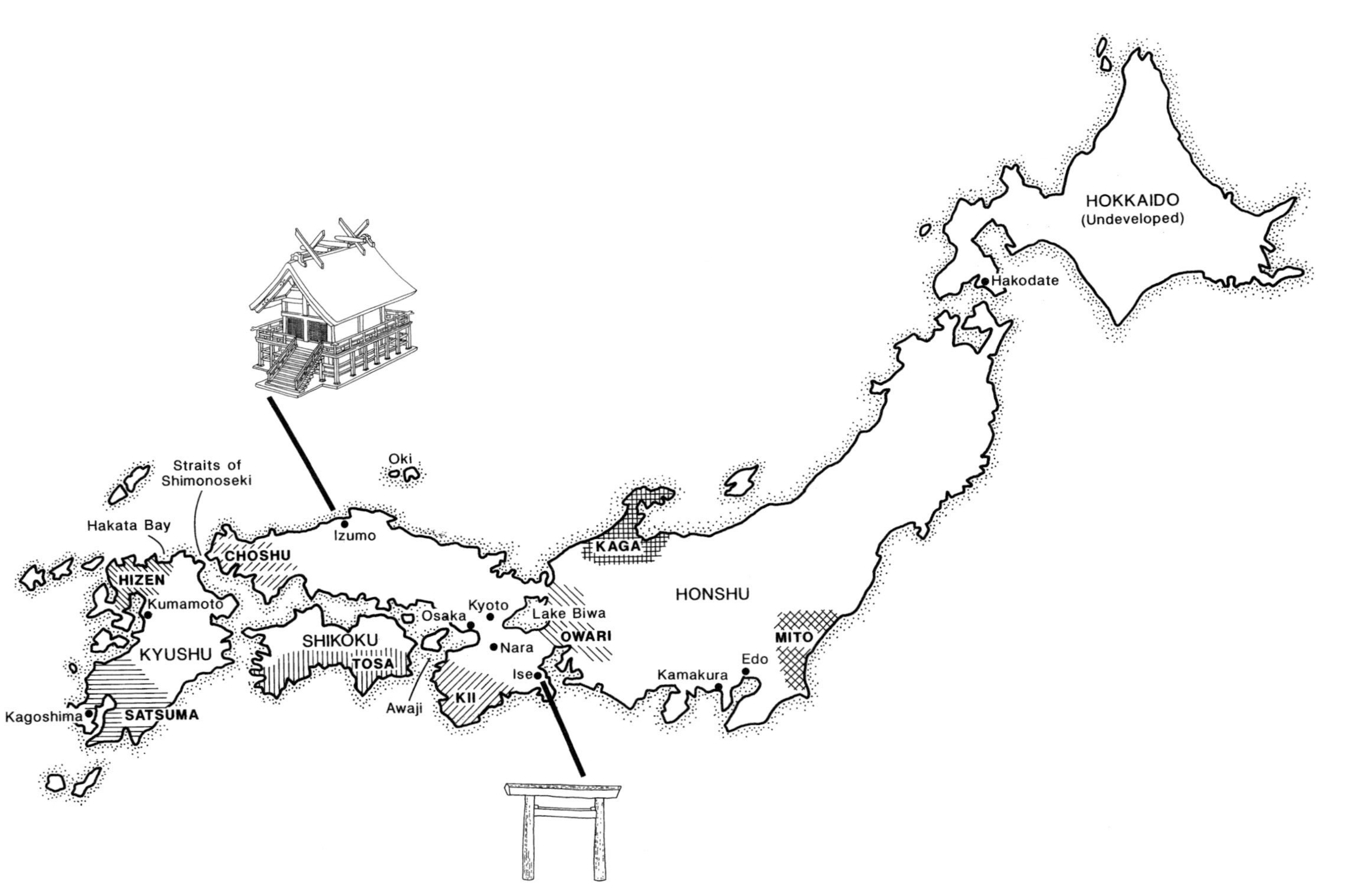

Japan in the early nineteenth century, showing feudal domains hostile to the Tokugawa shogunate

The Emperor Ninko

120. NINKŌ (1817–46)

Ninko was 18 when he succeeded his father, and he occupied the throne for nearly thirty years. Throughout his reign he took a keen interest in education. After his father died Ninko was responsible for establishing a school for nobles aged between 15 and 40, called at first the *Gakushujo* and later the *Gakushuin*, usually rendered in English as the Peers' School. (The foundation still exists, and though the peerage was abolished in 1945 it remains an immensely prestigious institution, one of whose famous alumni was the flamboyant novelist Yukio Mishima.) Partly as a consequence of the achievements of the school under imperial patronage, an influential party began to urge publicly the merits of an end to the dual system of government and a restoration of imperial authority. Paradoxically, one of its leading lights was Tokugawa Nariaki, a member of the ruling clan. Perturbed by the increasingly frequent breaches of the policy of seclusion which had endured for over two hundred years, Nariaki started organising the manufacture of cannon, and recommended other warlike preparations in defence of the realm. For his pains he was punished by being confined to Edo by the bakufu.

121. KŌMEI (1846–67)

Komei had been installed as crown prince in 1840, but was still not yet 15 when he came to the throne on the death of his father in 1846. Despite his youth, he soon displayed an awareness of the growing strength of the position he had inherited and the relative weakness of the failing shogunate, and was bold enough formally to notify the shogun Ieyoshi that he wished to be consulted on questions of foreign policy. Matters came to a head after this shogun's death and, hard upon it, the first of the American Commodore Perry's missions to Japan (in August 1853), when Perry lodged the formal request of the United States government to enter into treaty relations with Japan. After this démarche Perry departed, having informed the apprehensive bakufu officials that he would return in the following year to receive their response.

When he learned of this, the emperor firmly announced his refusal to make any concessions to the foreigners, but nevertheless Ii Naosuke, for the Edo government, ignored Komei's expressed views. When Perry duly returned, Ii and his colleagues told him that the American demands were accepted in principle, and negotiations followed. Between 1857 and 1859 the bakufu unilaterally concluded treaties of amity and commerce not only with the American negotiators, but also with representatives of the British, French and other governments, and agreed to open a number of Japanese ports to trade. Townsend Harris, newly arrived in Japan as the first American consul, was struck by the open disrespect for the emperor shown by high bakufu officials. In January 1858, he noted in his diary that '[The commissioners] spoke almost contemptuously of the Mikado, and roared with laughter when I quoted some remarks concerning the veneration in which he is held by the Japanese. They say he has neither money, political power, nor anything else that is valued in Japan. He is a mere cipher.'

Cipher or no, the Mikado had friends, and the imperial party was angered by these major political developments, though it was slow to move. Not until 1863 did Komei summon the new young shogun Iemochi (who had married his sister the previous year) to Kyoto, where he gave him a symbolic sword, and formally commanded him to expel the foreigners. The British in particular were then flexing their muscles, having inflicted great damage on the city of Kagoshima in the extreme south of Kyushu with a naval bombardment. This warlike act was one of retribution following the killing of a British national cut down by retainers of the *daimyo* of Satsuma for showing lack of respect to their lord, whose procession was passing on the highway. Kagoshima was the seat of government of the Satsuma clan.

In concert with their allies, the British also played a leading role in the shelling of another coastal city, Shimonoseki. This too was a retaliatory response, to the action of the *daimyo* of Choshu, in whose north Kyushu domain Shimonoseki was situated. He had ordered, in the name of the emperor, his shore batteries to fire on foreign ships as they passed through the straits. The foreign powers exacted a huge indemnity after the latter affair and, though there was much contention in the capital, at length Komei was induced to accept that resistance was useless and ratify the treaties which had been negotiated by Ii.

When the shogun Iemochi died, he was succeeded by the last person to hold that office. This was Keiki, the grandson of Nariaki, lord of Mito, from whom he may well have derived his own unusually deferential view of the imperial house. The stage was set for an imperial restoration, and it fell to Keiki (who lived on in respected retirement well into the twentieth century) to humbly request permission to surrender his political authority to the emperor. This was not Komei but his successor, for Komei died of smallpox in 1867. It is of historical interest that he was the last emperor of Japan whose funeral ceremony was conducted in accordance with Buddhist rites; obsequies in this long-established style for sovereigns, were, like so much else, abandoned and replaced by different forms during the extraordinary reign of his son. The arrival in Japan of representatives of the western powers clearly served as a catalyst, and produced an environment more conducive to change. But these events unfolded independently of outside intervention, at least to the extent that each of the powers (which backed different protagonists) made no overt attempt to influence developments in the political arena.

Komei's principal consort was Eisho (b. 1833), daughter of a senior nobleman, Kujo Naotada. She moved into the palace after the death of Ninko and bore Komei only one child, who did not survive infancy. He had five more children by other consorts, but only one of them lived to

The Empress Eisho

maturity, and he was the future emperor Meiji. Eisho became the boy's official mother, and after he succeeded to the throne Meiji bestowed on her the formal title of empress. Following the transfer of the court to Tokyo, and the construction of the new Akasaka Palace for the use of members of the imperial family other than the sovereign himself (who took over the former shogunal residence), Eisho lived there, taking a lively interest in the wonders of life outside the narrow confines of the court. She became a keen proponent of agricultural reform, often going to observe new techniques of cultivation at first hand, and she was an enthusiastic collector of western gadgets. The empress Eisho died in 1897, having lived long enough to see the status of the imperial house elevated to an extraordinary degree, and the child she had not borne, but who was regarded as her son, solemnly declared to be an *arahitogami*, or divinity in human form.

CHAPTER EIGHT

Reinventing the Monarchy

Brief reference has already been made to the *Dainihonshi* which Tokugawa Mitsukuni, the second *daimyo* of Mito, commissioned from the scholars collectively known as the Mito School. This was completed in 1720, so the downfall of those of his kinsmen who were at the titular head of the Tokugawa shogunate nearly a century and a half later can scarcely be laid to Mitsukuni's account. Nevertheless, the relevance of the *Dainihonshi* to the events of the mid-nineteenth century should not be underestimated. It was a dynastic history of Japan from mythical times up to the ending of the imperial schism in 1392, and there can be no doubt that it helped to stimulate a new climate of opinion which was theoretically unfavourable to the dual system of administration which had prevailed in various manifestations for the best part of a thousand years.

The collapse of the shogunate and the Meiji restoration have been seen by some western historians in simplistic terms as the inevitable outcome of the importunities and threats of the western powers, who breached the wall of Japanese national seclusion and made it clear that they would not tolerate the continuation of the policy of isolation which had served Japan rather well for two hundred years. Yet there were many in Japan who long before then foresaw the inevitable end of feudalism, and had begun to plot the course which they believed should be followed.

The political stability of the Tokugawa regime in its heyday rested on a complex accommodation between the demands and interests of two quite distinct groups of feudal lords or *daimyo* (literally 'great names'). The *fudai daimyo* were hereditary vassals of the shoguns, their fiefs in central, east and northern Japan having been derived from the Tokugawa clan by grant. Thus they were relatively biddable, and usually responsive to political pressure from above.

The position in the most westerly regions of the main island, Honshu, and in the islands of Shikoku and Kyushu was very different. The clans there were governed by men known formally as *tozama daimyo* or 'outsider lords', whose support for the central government had to be paid for, and who fostered fierce local patriotism in their domains. In the eighteenth and early nineteenth centuries the most powerful among these were the lords of the Satsuma and Saga clans in Kyushu, of Tosa in Shikoku, and of Choshu in the extreme south-west of Honshu and the northern tip of Kyushu. They were virtual kings in their territories, and they needed able young lieutenants to administer them. Most boys of the samurai class were literate by 1800, thanks to effective systems of education in place in each of the larger domains, and they were trained to be more useful with the writing brush and the abacus than with the sword, while those who displayed uncommon gifts were picked out for accelerated advancement. It was young men with this kind of background from the 'outsider' clans, most notably from Satsuma and Choshu, who constituted the pool of talent from which the political and military leaders of the Meiji era were drawn.

122. MEIJI (MUTSUHITO) (1867–1912)

Meiji, the only surviving child of the emperor Komei, was a youth of 15 at the time of his so-called restoration, and his early years had been spent within the stifling atmosphere of a shabby-genteel and inward-looking court, located in a capital which had seen better days. In the view of the American consul, Townsend Harris, in 1858,

> Kyoto is comparatively a poor place. The population, instead of being five hundred thousand as stated by Kaempfer (see above, p. 109), does not contain two hundred and fifty thousand. It is merely a city of priests and temples. No large manufactures are carried on, nor any lacquerware made there. Silk is not woven in more than twenty houses . . .

Meiji had been a mere child when his father Komei tried and failed to assert his authority over the shogunal government, whose effective leader, Ii Naosuke, had committed the nation to entering into treaty relations with the Great Powers. And when Komei's death was followed by the brief civil

The Emperor Meiji

war which resulted in a radical realignment of the whole system of the nation's government, it fell to this inexperienced youth to undertake the role of figurehead in a new order. Yet by the time of his death at the age of 60, the emperor Meiji had forged one of the most remarkable careers in the recorded history of Japan. He did so under the tutelage of the statesmen in whose hands the reins of power now rested; but they took the greatest pains to ensure that every decision was published in the name of the emperor, and to represent each one, no matter how trivial, as reflecting the imperial will.

Meiji's reign encompassed two distinct and sharply contrasting periods, between which the public image of the emperor was transformed. In the decade or so of enthusiasm for all things western immediately after the transfer of the capital from Kyoto to the former Edo, renamed Tokyo (eastern capital), Meiji was paraded as the very model of the modern sovereign. He usually appeared in full dress western military uniform, rode in open carriages in the full view of the cheering populace, undertook many public engagements such as visiting or opening exhibitions, and was promoted as an enlightened secular ruler like Queen Victoria or the Kaiser.

Feudalism was formally abolished. Men of the samurai class were required to give up wearing their two swords, and to abandon their distinctive hairstyle; they obeyed with surprisingly little demur. The new society was nevertheless far from classless. The old nobility, who traced their descent from the younger sons of former emperors and the families named in the ancient chronicles, were called in Japanese the *kuge.* They were now reinforced by amalgamation with the former *daimyo* and their immediate kin, all of them being assimilated into a peerage with a number of ranks in the European style. These Japanese princes, counts, barons and other grandees were collectively described as the *kazoku.* Generals were given impressive epaulettes and decorations, and senior politicians acquired titles.

As Oscar Wilde was famously to remark, 'the whole of Japan is a pure invention', and one of his elegant phrases from *The Importance of Being Earnest* might well also be applied to the 'new' nation: 'Every luxury that money can buy was lavished on her by her fond and doting parents.' Old Japan had no national flag: the Rising Sun emblem had been borrowed from one of the clans and adopted in 1860 by the embassy which sailed for the United States in that year on board the USS *Powhattan.* It was raised as the banner of the nation for the first time on Japanese soil twelve years later, when the emperor formally opened the first railway line, from Shinbashi in Tokyo to Yokohama. A military version, showing bold red rays streaming from the sun, was not long afterwards adopted by the army and navy. Old Japan lacked a national anthem before the Meiji restoration, so the *Kimigayo,* a poem from the tenth-century anthology *Kokinshu* was set to a traditional Japanese tune, and arranged for western instruments by the expatriate German bandmaster Franz Eckert; it was played in public for the first time on the occasion of the emperor's birthday in 1880. The musician Eckert was one of a virtual army of western experts hired by the new government at generous salaries to help equip Japan with all the appurtenances of a sophisticated and technically advanced society. It included specialists in jurisprudence from France, medical men from Germany, naval advisers, civil and railway engineers and scientists and

Internationalisation began in Japan during the Meiji period

teachers from Britain and the United States – besides others too numerous to mention.

In all this frenzy of updating, however, many of the old ways persisted in the imperial court. Particular honours were showered on Meiji's principal consort Shoken, who was two years younger than her husband and the daughter of a great noble, Ichijo Tadaka, head of one of the five houses whose origins could be traced back to the heyday of the Fujiwara. Shoken was the first imperial consort since 1285 to be accorded the title *Kogo*, or empress of the highest court rank. She presided over a domestic regime which in many ways resembled that which had prevailed for centuries past, for it was taken for granted that the emperor should openly have access to many other women who might also bear his children – children who would be recognised as being of the imperial blood.

Yet Shoken frequently emerged from the private apartments of the palace, and appeared in public almost as often as her husband, wearing fashionable dresses imported from Berlin. Like most European royal consorts, Shoken accompanied her husband on many of his official engagements. She attended balls with her ladies-in-waiting in the glittering western-style surroundings of the reception rooms in the fine red-brick building known as the Rokumeikan, which had been designed by the English architect Josiah Conder and was the centre of Tokyo's social scene. The imperial couple sat for official photographs, the young emperor – who could hardly be described as handsome – usually scowling, and his wife regally composed.

Little has yet been published about their private lives, but both Meiji and Shoken were renowned as prolific poets, the empress composing during her lifetime no fewer than thirty thousand *tanka*. Poetry has for well over a thousand years been regarded as an aristocratic pursuit in Japan, and has throughout that period been written and patronised by members of the imperial family. The bureau of poetry of the Imperial Household Agency still arranges the formal reading which is a prominent feature of the court's New Year observances. Even though each of the empress Shoken's poems consisted of only five lines, and the *tanka* form had in her time rigid conventions, with certain phrases recurring time and again, hers was no mean feat. Specimens of the imperial couple's poetry in their own elegant calligraphy are always displayed in the museum attached to the Meiji Shrine in Tokyo. Shoken bore some of Meiji's fourteen children, but her own all died in infancy. The empress was nevertheless regarded as the official mother of the only son of Meiji who survived. This was the future emperor Taisho, whose natural mother was Countess Yanagiwara Naruko, one of the twelve *koi* or official imperial concubines: ladies of the bedchamber in every sense.

The domestically traditional way of life and the superficially outgoing, up-to-date public personae of the emperor and his consort were to be transformed well before the turn of the century by a dramatic redefinition of the sovereign's status. The doctrine that Japanese emperors were divine may in an important sense be said to have been invented in the 1880s at the instigation of the statesman Count Ito, on his return from a visit he made to Count Otto von Bismarck. As the 'Iron Chancellor' who had been the architect of German unification, Bismarck knew a thing or two about fostering a sense of national identity, and he imparted his conclusions on the subject to his eager Japanese visitor. 'Bismarck's advice was this,' the veteran politician Count Okuma told the American journalist Willard Smith in 1915. 'Revive those parts of Shinto that exalt the authority and divinity of the emperor.' Whatever the degree of authenticity of this anecdote, there is no doubt that this is precisely the course followed by the late nineteenth-century Japanese oligarchs.

Shinto and the myth of the origins of Japan had of course already been revived. They had, in fact, never been forgotten; and though it lacked an ideological framework, Shinto was a vital factor in the shaping of the restoration. A proclamation of 5 April 1868 announced that 'henceforth the government will be based on a return to the Imperial Rule of Jimmu Tenno'; and on 22 April in the following year imperial envoys were sent to venerate the supposed tomb of the founding emperor, Jimmu. Three days after that, the young Meiji himself, with senior members of his court and representatives of the daimyos, took part in a solemn ceremony to worship all the gods of the Shinto pantheon and swear allegiance to the charter oath. This last was a short formulation of the aims and objectives of the new government, and had just been drawn up. In this first flush of enthusiasm a radical but doomed attempt was initiated to separate Shinto completely from the Buddhism with which it had become inextricably entwined over the centuries. Shinto priests who had simultaneously been in Buddhist orders were commanded to let their hair grow long as proof that they had renounced their affiliation with Buddhism. Buddhist priests who had, under the Tokugawa regime, been permitted to function as such in Shinto shrines were required either to return to secular life or to accept reordination as Shinto priests, in which case they were to start wearing Shinto vestments immediately. It was forbidden for the funeral services for these men or any member of their families to be conducted according to Buddhist rites. The pressure was maintained and even increased with the confiscation of all temple lands in February 1871, and the removal from the imperial palace precincts of all Buddhist statues and ritual objects and their transfer to a temple outside. This was accompanied by the abandonment of all the Buddhist ceremonies previously commissioned by the imperial household.

By the following year, the government had to accept that its policy of 'replacing' Buddhism by Shinto was causing serious social and political problems. Buddhism was deeply ingrained in the culture of Japan, and addressed itself to aspects of life which had not for well over a thousand years been regarded as the preserve of Shinto. Aggressive Christian missionaries made no secret of their hope that their own creed would replace Buddhism. The anti-Buddhist ordinances created more problems than they solved at almost every level, and were therefore quietly shelved for a decade. When Shinto was in the 1880s once again promoted by the authorities it was in a new, subtler guise: that of all-embracing emperor worship.

The forging of a national consciousness among people who had – particularly in the domains of the 'outsider lords' – a generation earlier thought of themselves as owing allegiance to their local *daimyo*, rather than to an emperor of whom the vast majority had possibly never heard, was going quite well. There were problems, of course. The architects of the Meiji restoration were not always of one mind, and the 1870s saw a number of attempts on the part of disgruntled individuals to challenge the policies of the new government.

The most serious of these was an armed rebellion led by a founding member of the oligarchy itself. He was a senior samurai from Satsuma called Saigo Takamori. Saigo was charismatic but vain; an opinionated and ambitious man who decorated his house with portraits of Napoleon I and III, Frederick the Great and Charlemagne. Collegiate government was never to his taste, and, when his recommendation that an invasion of Korea should be mounted was rejected by his colleagues, he resigned and exiled himself to Kyushu, where he waited in vain to be recalled to save the nation. In 1877 he was persuaded by some of his more romantic supporters there to take up arms against the Tokyo government. Against his own better judgement, and virtually disabled by kidney stones (like his hero Napoleon III), Saigo led a small army of disaffected samurai into battle at Kumamoto Castle. There he and his men were decisively defeated by government troops, and Saigo with a handful of his most loyal lieutenants retreated in disorder to the outskirts of the city of Kagoshima far to the south, where he protested his loyalty to the emperor Meiji and committed *seppuku*.

The taste for heroic failure which has always characterised the Japanese ensured that Saigo was posthumously rehabilitated, and a statue of him in informal Japanese dress, attended by his much-loved dog, today occupies a prominent site in Ueno Park in Tokyo. But all the same he lost. During the civil wars of the fifteenth and sixteenth centuries a cynical catchphrase was current: *kateba kangun* ('whichever side wins is the imperial army'). The humiliating defeat of Saigo emptied the phrase of meaning. Just a decade after the restoration, Japan now had but one modern national army, and though led by officers of samurai birth, it consisted in the main of peasant conscripts who had waged effective war in the name of their emperor.

A new, national patriotism had been born. Nevertheless, it was thought necessary for the people to be provided with an ideological framework which would reinforce their loyalty. Accordingly a new cult, which was designated State Shinto, was established at the behest of the Tokyo government. Ito and his associates and their staff resuscitated the mythology recounted by the court chroniclers of the eighth century and repeated by the Mito School a thousand years later. On their instructions, scholars and chamberlains investigated and codified in the minutest detail the ancient rituals relating to the throne and the sacerdotal duties of its occupant, the knowledge of which had been transmitted mainly through oral tradition and which had been revived sporadically since the civil strife of the fourteenth, fifteenth and sixteenth centuries. They added an extra dash of Confucianism, and tricked the mixture out to suit the exigencies of the time, much as King George V and his courtiers, in an attempt to 'keep the twentieth century at bay' were to reinvent the monarchy in Britain after the death of Edward VII.

Shinto priests were given salaries as minor civil servants, and for the first time were legally authorised to conduct marriage and funeral ceremonies. Buddhism, which had been patronised and promoted for more than twelve hundred years by emperors who routinely entered Buddhist orders after abdication and nominated their sons and daughters as abbots and nuns, was again forced to surrender some traditional privileges. In an extraordinarily short time the brand new Shinto wedding ceremony became the norm, and remains so throughout Japan. The consolations of Buddhism, however, continued to be sought by those in distress; virtually all funerals are still conducted according to its rites.

The emperor Meiji now disappeared from the view of the ordinary man and woman in the street, but in an abstract sense was omnipresent. The common people were required to hold in reverent awe a sovereign they were never permitted to set eyes on. When his closed carriage passed through the streets, all upper windows had to be shuttered so that nobody could look down from above on the vehicle containing his sacred person; and even those few courtiers and high officials permitted to enter his presence never raised their eyes to his. His clothes did not fit him very well, because no tailor could presume to run a tape measure over the physical manifestation of a living god, which was off-limits even to his physicians.

On the other hand, his photograph was the most venerated object in every school in the land. It was ritually displayed several times each year, when the Imperial Rescript on Education of 1890 was read aloud. This same rescript was hurriedly given a new but strictly temporary lease of life in late 1945 by Prince Higashikuni, Japan's first postwar prime minister, who with other members of the pre-war establishment put up a dogged but doomed rearguard action to keep it in force. It was well described by W.K. Bunce, one of General MacArthur's senior civilian advisers, as '. . . a Shinto-Confucianist document written for the purpose of keeping down "radical" (i.e. democratic) tendencies . . .'. The official English translation published at the time of its original promulgation ran as follows:

> Our Imperial Ancestors have founded our Empire on a basis broad and everlasting. Our subjects ever united in loyalty and filial piety have from generation to generation illustrated the beauty thereof. This is the glory of the fundamental character of Our Empire, and herein also lies the source of Our Education. Ye, Our Subjects, be filial to your parents, affectionate to your brothers and sisters; as husbands and wives be harmonious; as friends, true. Pursue learning and cultivate arts, and thereby develop intellectual faculties and perfect moral powers; furthermore, advance public good and promote common interests; always respect the Constitution and observe the laws; should emergency arise, offer yourselves courageously to the State; and thus guard and maintain the prosperity of Our Imperial Throne coeval with heaven and earth. So shall ye be not only Our good and faithful subjects, but render illustrious the best traditions of your forefathers.

> The Way here set forth is indeed the teaching bequeathed by Our Imperial Ancestors, to be observed alike by Their Descendants and the subjects, infallible for all ages and true in all places. It is Our wish to lay it to heart in all reverence, in common with you, Our subjects, that we may all thus attain to the same virtue.

The remarkable new cult of State Shinto was, designedly, never officially described as a religion, and was to endure for less than sixty years. Nevertheless, during that period it flourished mightily, and many westerners assume it to have ancient origins on that account. In terms of western logic and theology it was full of gaping holes. It was never clearly stated at what precise moment emperors became divine. Certainly not through the *Daijosai* ritual, which sometimes took place several years after the installation of a new incumbent on the throne. Nor was the status in Shinto terms of a crown prince or even a prince regent ever defined. During the years of Meiji's 'divinity', his son the future emperor Taisho appeared in public from time to time, and though his rank ensured that he was treated with enormous respect, until he succeeded his father it was never suggested that he was other than fully human. By the same token, during Taisho's own reign, divinity was never claimed for his son and heir Prince Hirohito. Even as prince regent he went about freely and was once photographed in the company of the visiting Prince of Wales in golfing attire complete with jaunty flat cap.

The awkward historical fact that so many past emperors had in their lifetimes become Buddhist priests was never explained or even referred to, and there cannot be much doubt that, however devoted they were to their sovereign, few intelligent Japanese were seriously deceived by the astonishing theories they had to pretend to swallow. Nevertheless, when he died, in the age of the motor car and the aeroplane, Meiji was mourned as a god, and his spirit is now enshrined in the huge Shinto complex erected in Tokyo to commemorate his reign, alongside that of his empress Shoken, who died two years after her husband and was the only Japanese woman ever to be officially apotheosised.

Whether or not Meiji himself was persuaded that he had, over a short period in the middle of his life, ceased to be a normal human being and become a god, he dutifully behaved in the manner deemed appropriate to his new role, and earned in political terms the status of father figure to his people. His son and heir, by contrast, constituted an extremely serious problem for the guardians of the new orthodoxy.

123. TAISHŌ (YOSHIHITO) (1912–26)

The emperor Taisho had been a sickly child, who early exhibited signs of serious mental instability as well as sadistic tendencies. Those charged with his upbringing did their best to conceal the physical and mental frailty of the crown prince and heir apparent – who in fact looked rather dashing as a young man – from all outside the innermost court circle, and a marriage was arranged when he was 20 years old. His 16-year-old bride was Sadako, who was a daughter of Prince Kujo Michitaka. Sadako was both intelligent and in excellent health. She had a tranquillising influence on her husband, bearing him four sons in all, the first a year after the wedding ceremony and the last in 1915, shortly before his final breakdown, after an effective separation which had lasted for more than ten years.

Taisho as a boy

Taisho as a young man

For several years Taisho as crown prince was able to undertake carefully supervised engagements, and in particular those which provided opportunities for him to indulge his taste for dressing up in military uniform. He was the first Japanese crown prince to travel outside the country, being taken on an official visit to Formosa (Taiwan), at that time and until 1945 under Japanese colonial rule. He was capable of stumbling through short formal speeches, and his hesitancy was not often noticed: Japanese dignitaries were and remain to this day poor orators.

The real test came after the death of Meiji. The new ideology demanded that the late emperor's funeral should be conducted according to Shinto rites, and that the protracted and elaborate rituals consequent on Taisho's accession should likewise be carried out meticulously. The mystical *Daijosai* rite during which the emperor was held to be in direct communion with the sun goddess Amaterasu herself, and which occupies more than one day and night, had to be postponed until the mourning ceremonies for the late emperor were complete. Then, having been set for November 1914, the ceremony was again put off, on account of the death of the late emperor's

The Empress Teimei, consort of Taisho

widow. It took place eventually a year later, and constituted such an ordeal for a sick man that it is widely believed to have led to Taisho's complete physical and mental breakdown. (There was to be an echo of this opinion twenty years later in Britain during the short reign of Edward VIII, when some informed observers asserted that the febrile new king would not be able to stand the strain of the coronation ceremony.)

The emperor Taisho was seen by all members of the government and many other politicians to be incapacitated when, at the formal opening of a session of the national Diet, he rolled the text of his speech into a tube and surveyed its members through it as though it were a telescope. The repercussions of such an episode in the television era are unimaginable; even then they amounted to a political disaster from the point of view of the government. In its aftermath the authorities faced a problem of their own making. In former times the obvious course would have been abdication, but this had been ruled out as recently as 1889 by the Imperial Household Law. Gods do not abdicate. The only course now open to the government was to arrange for Taisho to retire completely from his imperial duties, but technically to remain on the throne for the rest of his natural life, with his son the crown prince acting as his regent. Fortunately Prince Hirohito, who had recently returned from a successful European tour, was a robust young man of 20 in full possession of all his faculties, and late in 1921 the regency was proclaimed.

Taisho spent his last five years in seclusion, cared for by his principal consort Sadako, now the empress Teimei. Judging by a photograph of her in her maturity which survives, the empress was a very beautiful woman. She was also the mother of the first legitimate child of an emperor to succeed to the throne since Go-Momozono in the eighteenth century. In her long widowhood she displayed a wide and generous range of interests, and cultivated the acquaintance of appropriate westerners, notably that of the eccentric amateur scholar Richard Ponsonby-Fane, who was a devotee of the imperial house. So concerned was the dowager empress for the health of her friend that she knitted a woollen scarf for him. Ponsonby-Fane, overwhelmed by this token of imperial favour, wore it day in and day out until his death in 1938, by which time it had stretched to at least twice its original length; it reposed on top of his coffin during his funeral service. The empress Teimei survived until well after the Second World War, greatly loved by her grandson the present emperor.

CHAPTER NINE

Showa: Last of the Living Gods

124. SHŌWA (HIROHITO) (29 April 1901–7 January 1989: acceded 1926)

Countless books have been written about the Showa period, and a good many about the emperor who reigned for so long, and who was known to the world (and frequently vilified) as Hirohito. The Showa emperor has been variously portrayed as a war criminal, a reluctant tool of militarists bent on aggression, a shy, retiring amateur marine biologist of international distinction, a liberal who deplored the political regime of which he was the figurehead, and a lively-minded man who chafed under the constraints of the iron court protocol which governed virtually his every waking hour.

The isolated nature of his childhood is well documented. Separated from his parents when only three months old, the infant prince lived for three years in the household of an elderly senior courtier, the retired admiral Kawamura Sumiyoshi. Then the admiral died, and the prince, with his younger brother Chichibu, returned to the official residence of their parents the crown prince and princess. This was the Akasaka Palace, which is situated in its own park a considerable distance away from the enormous moated compound which for more than two hundred years housed the Tokugawa shoguns and now constitutes the grounds of the imperial palace. Rebuilt after the Second World War, the official home of the emperor and empress is an elegant but unpretentious range of buildings, comprising the residence proper and the emperor's offices. Nearby are those of the Imperial Household Agency; and sited discreetly out of view are the imperial Shinto shrines, including the *Kashikodokoro* which houses one of the items of the imperial regalia, the sacred jewel. A replica of the sword is also kept there. These shrines are where the emperor in his capacity as Shinto's *pontifex maximus* still celebrates a number of rituals, concerning which some details have never been published.

Hirohito (right) and his brother Chichibu as children

The Akasaka Palace to which the young princes were now moved stands in sharp contrast, not least because it was designed to resemble the palace of Versailles, if on a much more modest scale. (It is nowadays used as a secure guest-house for the accommodation of distinguished foreign guests of the Japanese government.) The boys did not live in the main palace building with their parents, but in a separate house in the extensive grounds. They were placed under the austere supervision of Kido Takamasa, another grandee of samurai origins, until Hirohito was seven, when he was enrolled in the Peers' School. There he came under the quasi-paternal care of its principal, Count Marusuke Nogi, a retired general who had, as a young man, fought in the imperial cause in the brief civil war of 1867 which ushered in the Meiji era. Decades later Nogi had been the general commanding the Third Japanese Army in the Russo-Japanese war (1905–6), in which two of his sons were killed. Obviously, the second in line of succession to the imperial throne would in any case have been given very particular attention at school, but it does seem that a remarkable personal rapport developed between the old man and the young boy.

When Hirohito was eleven years old his grandfather Meiji died, and his status immediately changed to that of heir apparent to his father, the new emperor Taisho. On the eve of the funeral of the late emperor, Nogi summoned the prince his protégé, and for three hours examined him on his progress in calligraphy and other subjects. After dismissing him with words of approval and encouragement, Nogi proceeded to his house, where he and Countess Nogi committed ritual suicide. He had been a senior samurai in imperial service, and this was his last act of fealty to his old master Meiji, and hers to her husband. Though Hirohito was throughout his long life never known to allude to the suicides, the news of them caused a sensation in the press. There was much comment about the stately, traditional manner in which the count and countess went to their deaths. In the opinion of many historians, such classical samurai behaviour tended not only to revivify and glorify the cluster of feudal beliefs and practices known as bushido or the way of the warrior, but linked them with the imperial throne manifestly and disastrously, as subsequent events were to show. Count Nogi, the old soldier, died spectacularly for his sovereign Meiji, and his example was to be cited in justification of the slogans current during the Second World War encouraging countless soldiers, sailors, airmen and civilian men, women and children to sacrifice their lives in the name of Meiji's grandson.

Responsibility was heaped early on the young prince. At the age of 15 he was formally installed as crown prince, and as such was no longer known as Prince Hirohito, but by the arcane title *Togu* ('Eastern Palace') or less obscurely as *Kotaishi* ('the Crown Prince'). Taisho's precarious state of health made the question of the future succession a matter of urgency, and discussions were opened in high government and court circles with the objective of identifying a suitable bride for the emperor-in-waiting. It was taken for granted at first by one of those involved, the aged and opinionated statesman Prince Yamagata, that a young woman from his own Choshu nobility would be selected. However, the empress Teimei, when she heard of Yamagata's expectations, made her strong objections to this idea known. She was backed by influential supporters such as the Lord Privy Seal, Count Makino (a senior adviser to the throne and a member of the Satsuma nobility who had his own candidate in mind) and Professor Sugiura, an eminent academic who as one of his appointed tutors taught ethics to the young prince. Makino's own nominee was his young relative Princess Nagako, daughter of Prince Kuniyoshi Kuni. Her name was put to the crown prince, Nagako found imperial favour, and their engagement was announced early in 1918.

Extraordinarily, Yamagata refused to admit defeat, and embarked on a long and demeaning campaign to frustrate the marriage. His personal physician dredged up an obscure article in a medical journal which traced a history of colour-blindness in Nagako's mother's family, and Yamagata even attempted to buy her father off. His scheming became a public scandal, and was seen to have been fruitless when the ailing emperor himself, on being told about the matter, offered no objection to the marriage. Accordingly, the engagement was officially confirmed in 1921. (It later transpired that Nagako, a keen amateur painter in watercolours, was not in fact colour-blind, but nobody had thought to arrange for her vision to be tested before the public fuss was raised.)

Before his wedding the crown prince was given what was to him an exhilarating taste of comparative freedom in the form of a tour of Europe. He visited Scotland, and in London was invited to stay at Buckingham Palace, being received there by King George V, who had presided over the less sweeping, but in the long term more enduring, reinvention of the British monarchy. To the prince's astonished pleasure, George V wandered into his apartments one morning in his shirt-sleeves and braces for a private conversation. His stay in Buckingham Palace gave the crown prince a taste for the conventional English breakfast, which he elected to eat nearly every day for the rest of his life. Hirohito next went to Paris, which proved even more of an eye-opener for him: he was taken to nightclubs, attended parties, and handled money for the first and probably the last time in his life, when he paid for his own Metro ticket.

Back in Japan, he welcomed the Prince of Wales for a reciprocal visit, took him sightseeing in Kyoto and Nara, and waved to the crowds of his future subjects who gathered to catch a glimpse of the two young men. He

Hirohito with the then Prince of Wales

The Emperor Showa and Empress Nagako

had by then become prince regent, and such informal behaviour shocked the imperial chamberlains, but he did not seem to be abashed. On the contrary, some time later he invited a number of his former Peers' School classmates to a western-style evening party at the Akasaka Palace. Musicians capable of playing dance music and jazz were engaged, and the regent genially urged his boyhood friends to forget about protocol for the evening.

The occasion was a deeply embarrassing disaster, for what was normal and natural behaviour for privileged young men and women in Europe proved alien and unacceptable to the Japanese. Saddened and chastened by the failure of his attempt to inject some gaiety into life at court, the prince admitted defeat and took such personal comfort as he could in the prospect of his impending marriage to Princess Nagako. This took place in January 1924, the catastrophic Kanto earthquake of 1923 having necessitated a postponement from the date originally set.

The Empress Nagako in her enthronement robes

Little more than two years later, on 25 December 1926, the young man became emperor. He was 25 years old, fit and vigorous, being a particularly strong swimmer; and was extremely happy in his marriage. Six healthy children were born to Nagako during the ensuing decade. The only problem was that the first four were daughters, which we know from diaries kept by members of his household troubled the imperial couple not at all, but greatly alarmed senior courtiers anxious about the succession. They went so far as to counsel the emperor to emulate his grandfather Meiji and appoint concubines, in the hope of begetting a son, but he angrily brushed aside the very idea. In the event, Nagako did not disappoint even the most pessimistic of the chamberlains: there was general public rejoicing when she bore a son in December 1933, and it was renewed when her sixth and last child proved also to be a boy (Prince Hitachi).

Whatever the State Shinto ideologists asserted, the Showa emperor thought of himself as a constitutional monarch, bound in principle to act on the advice of his ministers. (He had come to maturity during a decade in which speech was relatively free and party politics were lively; it was

The Emperor Showa and Empress Nagako

known as 'Taisho democracy'.) Nevertheless there were three memorable occasions during his long reign when he acted decisively and independently. The first related to the notorious incident of 4 June 1928, which took place just outside Mukden, the Manchurian capital. The *de facto* ruler of Manchuria at the time was the warlord Chang Tso-lin. Chang had been useful to the Japanese military forces in the area (the so-called Kwantung army) for more than twenty years, since the end of the Russo-Japanese wars. He was, however, currently being hard pressed by his enemy Chiang Kai-shek, and had thus become an embarrassment to the Kwantung army command, who regarded themselves as sovereign in the region. Arrangements were therefore made for his assassination, which was stage-managed by a senior officer, Colonel Komoto. The official line, that Chang had fallen victim to Chinese guerrillas, proved too flimsy to sustain, and a major political row broke out. Under pressure, the prime minister, Tanaka, agreed to order an enquiry into the incident, and more generally into the arrogant and indisciplined behaviour of the Kwantung army.

Some six months later Tanaka confessed to the emperor, promising that punitive disciplinary measures would be taken against the colonel and others responsible. Yet in the event, Komoto and his superior, the general commanding the Kwantung army, were simply removed from the active service list.

Tanaka reported this personally to the emperor more than a year after the incident had taken place. The emperor was furious, accusing the prime minister outright and in unusually blunt language of having lied to him. This unprecedented imperial rebuke involved such loss of face for Tanaka that he had no option but to resign in disgrace, with his entire cabinet following suit. In the political aftermath the emperor leant heavily on the disinterested advice of the elder statesman Prince Saionji, who mistrusted the militarists and recommended that the leader of the other major party in the Diet (hardly an 'opposition' as the term is generally understood) should succeed Tanaka as prime minister.

The fact that the emperor had personally brought about a change of administration in the interests of openness was a notable contribution to the preservation of the decencies of civil government which had prevailed since the death of Meiji. Unfortunately, however, the arrangement whereby the posts of army and navy minister had to be filled by senior officers on the active list remained in force, and the high-handed style and political ambitions which characterised the Kwantung army gradually infected the forces based in Japan itself. This was manifested through an organisation called the Young Officers' Movement, which was viewed with avuncular indulgence by a significant number of highly placed generals.

What had begun as an informal political debating club (which in its early days enjoyed the support of the emperor's younger brother Prince Chichibu, an army major) developed into a tightly knit organisation of passionately idealistic junior officers. They planned to 'liberate' the emperor from the clutches of what they saw as a sinister combination of capitalist business interests, unpatriotic liberal politicians and reactionary courtiers; and to free the army to save the nation in his name. They referred to their programme as 'The Imperial Way'. In the early hours of 26 February 1936, about three dozen lieutenants and captains made their move, deploying some 1,500 soldiers of the Tokyo garrisons, and staging an attempted coup d'état in the capital, seizing a number of government buildings and publishing their manifesto. At the same time small teams were sent out to assassinate the prime minister, the finance minister, a senior general, Watanabe, who was strongly opposed to their ideas, Count Makino, an adviser second only to Prince Saionji in the emperor's estimation, and the Lord Privy Seal, Viscount Saito. Saito, Finance Minister Takahashi and General Watanabe were murdered in their beds. The prime minister escaped only because the assassins did not know what he looked like, and killed his brother-in-law by mistake, while Count Makino, who was staying at a hot-spring resort not far from Tokyo, was enabled to elude the men sent to kill him through the bravery and presence of mind of his young granddaughter, who was with him.

The reckoning was slow in coming. For three days the general in command of the Tokyo garrison hesitated, aware that the ringleaders had the tacit support of some members of the Imperial General Staff, while others sat on the fence. The admirals, however, were of a different mind, and deployed warships in Tokyo Bay in support of the government. For two or three days there was stalemate, and there can be no doubt that the man who did most to frustrate the coup was the emperor. Beside himself with anger at the news of the assassinations, he summoned the army minister and chief of the general staff to his presence and berated them, denouncing the coup organisers as treasonous mutineers. Ordering that the rising should be put down forthwith, he made it plain that the officers who had led it should without delay be arraigned before courts-martial, and suffer condign punishment.

This, the emperor's second independent initiative, was even more effective than his first had been six years earlier. On a number of previous occasions officers had faced military tribunals to answer for politically motivated acts, including assassinations. They had, however, been treated indulgently, being permitted to make long political statements which were given the wide press coverage they sought for their views. Even when found guilty they had been metaphorically slapped on the wrist, by having token sentences passed on them. This time the emperor personally insisted that the trials should be conducted quickly and according to the letter of military law, without speeches on the part of the accused, and without publicity. His orders were obeyed, and within weeks fifteen of the officers were condemned to death by firing squad, the sentences to be carried out without delay. The only concession to their rank was that the members of the firing squads, uniquely, were all volunteer junior officers. The young men faced their peers proudly and without flinching, and their last utterances were cries of 'Long Live The Emperor!'

During the years of the war in China and, later, the world war, the emperor as commander-in-chief formally reviewed his troops from time to time, notably at New Year, on the great parade ground which was, two decades later, to become the site of the 1964 Tokyo Olympic Village. He was usually mounted on the pure white Lippizaner charger whose name, *Shirayuki* or 'White Snow', was famous throughout the empire. There is no evidence that these ceremonial martial duties were distasteful to him. His personal way of life, however, was in total contrast. He spent as much time as possible in private at the spartan imperial villa by the beach in the village of Hayama at Sagami Bay. This modest house lacked even a telephone, but it did boast a simple laboratory. There the emperor pursued his consuming interest in marine biology, going out in a small boat in search of specimens and often swimming, escorted at a deferential distance by at least two chamberlains.

Controversy about the emperor's share of responsibility for the Pacific war will probably never cease. He had shown on at least two occasions that he could and would intervene decisively in political affairs when sufficiently angry. Yet this very intelligent, thoughtful man remained passive after 1936 as the drift to war continued. It has been argued that after the attack on Pearl Harbor, the emperor was virtually a prisoner of his ministers, only selectively informed about the course of the war, and with no role in its conduct. He no doubt rejoiced in Japan's early military triumphs, and was depressed when within less than a year they were nullified by the inexorable advance of the Allied, mostly American, forces. When the unthinkable happened and American aircraft bombed Tokyo itself, the emperor was urged to leave his capital. He refused. Then, as defeat began to seem not only probable but inevitable, senior figures in the government had to contemplate the ultimate horror: the arraignment before foreign judges of the Son of Heaven as a war criminal, followed by a trial and a death sentence.

Wild schemes were hatched to frustrate such a possibility, and one was actually initiated. Prince Konoe went to Kyoto (which was largely spared attack from the air) and had a confidential meeting with the abbot of the Zen Buddhist temple complex of Ninna-ji there. That dignitary was persuaded that if he were to step down, the emperor might, in spite of the law which by then ruled out such a step, abdicate and enter Buddhist orders in order to succeed him as abbot. Preposterous as the idea was, a precedent could be found: the emperor Uda (59) had done precisely that, becoming abbot of Ninna-ji in AD 897. On Konoe's return to Tokyo the suggestion was finally broached to the emperor; he predictably turned it down flat.

Atomic bombs annihilated the city of Hiroshima and wrought terrible destruction in Nagasaki, and defeat was now imminent. Showa's third major political initiative was taken at the humble request of his divided Supreme War Council, who begged him to make the decision they were unable to agree on. As is well known, the emperor opted for surrender and peace, and personally recorded the broadcast message which conveyed his decision to his people.

The dramatic story of the imperial radio broadcast, and of the convoluted, archaic language in which it was couched, has often been told. Not many of the millions of Japanese who heard it on the wireless sets of the time could understand the Voice of the Crane, which had to be interpreted for them in the vernacular. When the message was finally absorbed, crowds of people flocked to the plaza of the imperial palace, and a considerable number committed suicide, some by ritual *seppuku*.

But the war was over, and it was the end of an era. To the 'Three Initiatives' recorded in the history books should, however, be added two more. A month after the broadcast, in September 1945, the emperor called at his own request on General Douglas MacArthur, supreme commander of the Allied forces in Japan, at his residence in Tokyo. There he told MacArthur that he accepted responsibility for every act committed in his name during the war; this was his fourth and personally bravest independent action as emperor.

The fifth and last was the most spectacular. On New Year's Day 1946 the emperor issued a formal rescript, in which he repudiated any claim to divinity. On this occasion his words were forthright and specific, and their meaning clear:

> The ties between us and our people have always stood upon mutual trust and affection. They do not depend upon mere legends and myths. They are not predicated on the false conception that the Emperor is divine and that the Japanese people are superior to other races and fated to rule the world.

With these words, less than a century after Meiji was, in his middle age, transformed into a god, his middle-aged grandson ceased to be one.

CHAPTER TEN

The Monarchy Deconstructed

The question of what to do about the emperor was hotly debated by interested parties, both before and after the Japanese surrender to the Allied powers in 1945. A number of regional military tribunals were set up in areas occupied by Japanese forces during the war, and these dealt in summary fashion with a great many individuals charged with war crimes, including senior commanders. The principal focus of media interest, however, was the international court convened in Tokyo to hear the cases of the Japanese leaders regarded as having been primarily responsible for the war. It was equipped with an appropriately distinguished panel of eleven judges, one each from the United States, Australia, New Zealand, the United Kingdom, China, France, Canada, the Philippines, India, the Netherlands and the Soviet Union. Thus only the victors sat in judgement on the vanquished. There were no representatives of neutral powers such as Switzerland, much less an appointed Japanese observer. These omissions troubled only Judge Pal of India, who expressed his profound dissatisfaction, and Judge Roling of the Netherlands, who made it clear that he was unhappy about aspects of the constitution and terms of reference of the tribunal. Sir William Webb of Australia, who was appointed president of the tribunal, seems at first to have been under the impression that it was for him and his colleagues on the bench to decide who among the wartime leaders of Japan should stand trial. He made no secret of his personal opinions on the subject of the emperor, who was in his view obviously the war's prime mover and evil genius, and should therefore be the first to appear in the dock, with his prime minister Tojo by his side.

What Sir William and others of like mind failed to understand was that the new ruler of Japan was General Douglas MacArthur, who had no intention of casting the emperor in the role of war criminal. On the contrary, he had by the middle of September 1945 already described him as 'the first gentleman of Japan'. For MacArthur and his favoured advisers, the emperor had been throughout his reign *above* politics, and could no more be held to account for war crimes committed in his name than King George VI was personally to blame for the saturation bombing of Dresden by the Royal Air Force. Quite apart from that, geopolitical considerations dominated the American agenda. The Soviet Union had declared war on Japan a few days before the capitulation, and was therefore technically one of the victorious Allies, looking for a share in the spoils. The preservation of the imperial institution in Japan was seen as being vital to the American strategic interest, while in the short term it was viewed as essential if civic order was to be maintained in the aftermath of defeat, and a communist takeover avoided.

The emperor's initiative in formally renouncing on New Year's Day 1946 the claims to divinity made for his grandfather Meiji, his father Taisho and for himself might, on the face of it, seem to have made him more vulnerable to legal attack; but in fact it paved the way for the imposition on a reluctant civilian government and national Diet of the new, American-inspired 'peace' constitution of 1947, which declared that the emperor was not the head, but merely the 'symbol' of a democratic state, with the same personal rights under the law as ordinary citizens.

The emperor was never arraigned, and there was no interruption in his tenure of the throne. The imperial lifestyle was, however, transformed. The duties assigned to him in time of peace were purely ceremonial. He retained his title, as did his mother, his brothers and their wives, his own wife the empress and his two sons; but his four daughters ceased to be princesses on marriage and became commoners, as did members of the former peerage, now abolished. Over seven thousand employees of the imperial household lost their jobs, and the remaining members of the new, much reduced imperial family were deprived of their personal fortunes and in effect placed on the government payroll, with adequate but by no means extravagant financial provision being made for them.

They were expected to undertake public relations work for their keep. In the immediate postwar years the emperor and his closest relatives busied themselves by going about the country and meeting ordinary people, undertaking charitable duties, and showing that they were living relatively simple personal lives. The emperor's own daily round took him to factories, coal-mines and other workplaces. He cut innumerable ribbons to open exhibitions in galleries and department stores, and attended baseball games, *sumo* tournaments and other public events. He never failed to raise his hat politely and offer a few stilted remarks to those he met. It amounted to a strenuous programme of retraining; he was awkward and shy in such unfamiliar surroundings and had never been taught how to make small-talk. He became famous for one phrase which he invariably used when told anything: '*Ah, so desu-ka?*', which means 'Is that so?' Before long the emperor was popularly known as 'Mr Is-That-So', and MacArthur as 'the blue-eyed shogun'; but the currency of the tags was evidence of respect and even, perhaps, of some new-minted affection, and the press in all its heady freedom soon found that the private lives and behaviour of the members of the reduced imperial family were irreproachable.

After the Occupation came to an end and Japan became effectively a sovereign state again, the emperor retreated once more into a more private way of life. His youngest brother Prince Mikasa, a university professor who never hesitated to speak his mind, complained wryly that a chrysanthemum curtain had descended once more on the head of the family. The truth was, rather, that the emperor had grown weary of public life, and thankfully immersed himself in his research into marine biology. He achieved genuine distinction in the field, publishing a number of scholarly papers, and a book about a new species of shrimp which he had discovered. But he scrupulously performed his limited public duties, and, usually in strict privacy, performed certain Shinto rites in his priestly role. Just one of these annual rituals was much publicised. Every year photographs would appear in the press depicting the emperor in shirt-sleeves and a panama hat, his trousers tucked into rubber boots, stooping down to transplant seedlings into a small, waterlogged rice field within the palace precincts. The rice harvested in due course from this field would be used to provide the votive offerings at the imperial shrines.

Showa did not become a recluse. Far from it: he was the first reigning emperor of Japan to travel overseas, exactly half a century after the European tour he had undertaken as crown prince and which he always described as the happiest experience of his life. He visited the London Zoo,

Prince Akihito receiving instruction in English from Elizabeth Gray Vining

where, being a well-informed scientist, he asked its staff tricky questions; and almost to the end of his days he often teased his strait-laced chamberlains by wearing the Mickey Mouse watch he had been given in Disneyland in Florida. Ordinary Japanese flocked in their thousands to the imperial palace precincts at New Year to wave paper Rising Sun flags and cheer the diminutive figure who appeared on a balcony at intervals with his wife and children and diffidently acknowledged their greetings. The world was spared few of the dismal physical details of his last illness, and his death on 7 January 1989 set off a rush to judgement on a man who had by any reckoning lived an extraordinary life, and who alone knew whether or not he deserved to have been in the dock with his senior wartime servants.

125. HEISEI (AKIHITO) (b. 23 December 1933: acceded 1989)

Prince Akihito, Showa's elder son, was born three years before the attempted coup d'état of 1936, in the face of which his father showed such angry decisiveness. As a small child he was sheltered and excluded from the political world, and was still only twelve years old when the war ended. Then, early in 1946, his father made a decision which was to transform his young life: he appointed Elizabeth Gray Vining to be Akihito's personal tutor. Mrs Vining was an American and a Quaker, who exhibited all the generous but firm principles characteristic of members of the Society of Friends. She was modest about her abilities, never pretending to be a towering intellectual, but was nevertheless confident in her mission, which she summed up in the title of her memoir, *Windows for the Crown Prince.* She was a member of the imperial household for only four years, but her influence, not only upon her charge but also upon his siblings and more senior relatives, not excluding the empress and the emperor himself, was enormous and lasting. She even persuaded senior officials at the Imperial Household Agency to relax their iron grip on imperial protocol just a little.

Mrs Vining took up her duties in October 1946, and throughout her stay in Japan Prince Akihito attended the Peers' School, in Tokyo and later at its middle school campus at Koganei, over an hour's drive away. The school buildings there were shabby and austere, and bitterly cold in winter. The boy had his own house on the campus, where he lived for most of each week in term time, being attended night and day by his own chamberlains. Ironically, the building in which Mrs Vining met him for their private English lessons was the *Kokaden* or Pavilion of Glorious Light, which had originally been erected on the plaza of the imperial palace in Tokyo in 1940 to house some of the celebrations of the 2,600th 'anniversary' of the legendary emperor Jimmu's inauguration.

Mrs Vining was not the sort of woman to be overwhelmed by this resonant environment. When attending her general classes in English with his fellow pupils, Prince Akihito along with all the others had to answer to a western nickname bestowed by his teacher. Mrs Vining chose to call him 'Jimmy', which was either a singularly happy coincidence, or evidence of a sly sense of humour in the woman who regularly met him in a building designed to honour his near namesake Jimmu.

By the time the Occupation ended in 1952 the prince was, in his father's view, ready to assume a public role. He was installed as crown prince and heir apparent in November of that year, and was very soon to be tested in the lessons he had learned from Mrs Vining, by travelling overseas to represent Japan at the coronation of Queen Elizabeth II in London in 1953. This he did with tact and grace at a time and in a place where there was little public respect for his country.

In 1958 the crown prince met (on a tennis court) and soon fell in love with Michiko Shoda, a young woman with a rich father but without aristocratic connections. Doubts about her suitability were hinted at in court circles, but the crown prince had the support of his parents and the engagement was announced in November. The press and the people were enthusiastic, and the period leading up to the wedding four months later saw an unprecedented degree of publicity for the imperial family. The marriage proved to be both happy and fruitful, and when their two sons and their daughter were younger they shared with their parents a love of music, and formed their own domestic chamber ensemble.

As a liberated, sensitive young woman with a degree in English literature who had enjoyed an active social life, the new crown princess found the constraints of her new life hard to cope with, and it is well known that during the thirty-eight years of her marriage the empress Michiko has suffered more than one nervous breakdown. There can be no doubt that

Crown Prince Akihito with Michiko Shoda before their marriage

when her elder son the present crown prince (himself, like his brother, having experienced postgraduate life at Oxford University) wished to marry a commoner like his father before him, the empress understood from her own bitter experience the well-publicised reluctance of the young woman concerned to forfeit her personal freedom by joining the imperial family. And what is the state of that family as the twentieth century draws to a close?

At the time of the Osaka International Exposition in 1970 there were three emperors in the world: the Shah of Iran, the Emperor of Ethiopia and the Emperor of Japan. All three visited Expo '70; and all three are now dead. There are no longer imperial thrones of Iran or Ethiopia, but that of Japan survives. The Japanese imperial institution is an extraordinary phenomenon. Even discounting its legendary origins, its durability has been comparable to that of the Vatican, and is many times greater than that of any other monarchical dynasty in recorded history. Given that the majority of the emperors of Japan since the eighth century have been politically powerless, that many of them were children and that others lived and died in poverty, what possible reason can there be to account for the demonstrable fact that, for at least fifteen hundred years, members of a single kinship group have been granted unique status in a society in which almost everything else has changed? Japan's economy has moved from an agricultural basis to one geared to a high degree of industrialisation and international financial and commercial activity. The common people have experienced life under local warlords, a feudal order, a totalitarian nationalist regime, militarist adventures and, latterly, as much democracy as is to be found in any other developed nation.

Temporal power frequently changed hands, yet the most ruthlessly ambitious contenders invariably sought the cloak of legitimacy; and the source of that legitimacy throughout the recorded history of Japan was until our own times the imperial institution. Frequent reference has been made to the Japanese taste for indirect rule, and the repeated development of apparently illogical systems within which hereditary office-holders relinquish their executive powers to deputies, who themselves assume hereditary status and delegate their authority to others. Wildly irrational it might appear, but it has given to the body politic which is Japan a degree of continuity and an essential stability which may be thought of as a product of collectively unconscious ingenuity.

Constitutionally, the imperial throne is no longer the source of legitimacy. It has been replaced in theory by the will of the people. Is it likely that they will eventually decide that emperors belong to history and not to the future? That the continued existence of the oldest monarchical house in the world will come into question as that of the House of Windsor in Britain has done in recent years? It has to be said that there is little evidence of popular dissatisfaction with the present low-profile imperial institution. Nor is there widespread yearning to put the clock back, except on the part of a few diehard traditionalists. These do, however, include a number of influential politicians and officials. Officials of the Imperial Household Agency today are heirs to a culture of intense conservatism. This manifests itself in relatively harmless ways; in spite of the refreshing

Emperor Akihito

legacy of Elizabeth Gray Vining's hard-won battles, they cling obstinately to the minutiae of protocol, and senior members of the imperial family are known to suffer in this claustrophobic environment.

Of greater political concern is the fact that some at least of the chamberlains, like many right-wing politicians, are even after half a century unreconciled to the passing of the old ideology; and leading members of the government continually edge towards the boundaries of the permissible in regard to the status of Shinto in relation to the state and the imperial family.

The process began even under the Occupation, when the then civil government fought a passionate but ultimately unsuccessful rearguard action to prevent the rescinding of the Meiji emperor's rescript on education. In 1953 the shrines at Ise were renewed, not after the traditional twenty years, but for the first time since 1929 (the twenty-year cycle was restored with the next renewals, in 1973 and 1993 respectively).

Most significantly of all, the essential elements in the funeral of the Showa emperor in 1989 were conducted in accordance with Shinto ritual, the constitutional decencies of a secular state being respected – just – by concealing these rites from the sight of the international dignitaries who were present as government guests. And the present emperor's coronation ceremonies included the mystical *Daijosai* communion rituals. These took place not in Kyoto, but in the East Garden of the imperial palace in Tokyo from 22 to 25 November 1990. The present emperor is a liberal, enlightened man with both scientific and broad cultural interests, but he is sensitive to the historical continuity of his sacerdotal role. Few predictions about the future of the monarchy in Japan can be made with confidence, save one: that its passing would end not an era but a unique historical tradition.

The present emperor should have the last word: in the form of the authorised English translation of one of his published poems. It was written in 1970, after he took part as crown prince in a Shinto court ceremony:

Walking
Along the verandah
Lit by torches,
I find myself
Thinking of ancient times

The Traditional List of Emperors and Empresses Regnant

	Posthumous name	*Born*	*Acceded*	*Abdicated*	*Died*
A: LEGENDARY EMPERORS					
1.	JIMMU		660 BC		585
2.	SUIZEI	632	581		549
3.	ANNEI	577	549		511
4.	ITOKU	553	510		477
5.	KŌSHŌ	506	475		393
6.	KŌAN	427	392		291
7.	KŌREI	342	290		215
8.	KŌGEN	273	214		158
9.	KAIKA	193	158		98
10.	SUJIN	148	98		30
11.	SUININ	69	29		AD 70
12.	KEIKŌ	13	AD 71		130
B: PREHISTORICAL EMPERORS (ALL DATES UNRELIABLE)					
13.	SEIMU	AD 84	131		190
14.	CHŪAI	149	192		200
15.	ŌJIN	200	270		310
16.	NINTOKU	257	313		399
17.	RICHŪ	319	400		405
18.	HANZEI	351	406		410
19.	INGYŌ	376	412		453
20.	ANKŌ	401	453		456
21.	YŪRYAKU	418	456		479

Posthumous name		*Born*	*Acceded*	*Abdicated*	*Died*
22.	SEINEI	444	479		484
23.	KENZŌ	450	485		487
24.	NINKEN	449	488		498
25.	BURETSU	489	498		506

C: HISTORICAL EMPERORS AND EMPRESSES REGNANT (ER)

26.	KEITAI	450	507	531	531
27.	ANKAN	466	531		536
28.	SENKA	467	536		539
29.	KIMMEI	509	539		571
30.	BIDATSU	538	572		585
31.	YŌMEI	540	585		587
32.	SUSHUN	521	587		592
33.	SUIKO (ER)	554	593		628
34.	JOMEI	593	629		641
35.	KŌGYOKU (ER)	594	642	645	
36.	KŌTOKU	596	645		654
37.	SAIMEI* (ER)		655		661
	(* previously reigned as Kogyoku)				
38.	TENJI	626	668		671
39.	KŌBUN	648	671		672
40.	TEMMU	622	673		686
41.	JITŌ (ER)	645	690	697	702
42.	MOMMU	683	697		707
43.	GEMMEI (ER)	661	707	715	721
44.	GENSHŌ (ER)	680	715	724	748
45.	SHŌMU	701	724	749	756
46.	KŌKEN (ER)	718	749	758	
47.	JUNNIN	733	758	764	765
48.	SHŌTOKU* (ER)		764		770
	(* previously reigned as Koken)				
49.	KŌNIN	709	770	781	781
50.	KAMMU	737	781		806

Posthumous name		*Born*	*Acceded*	*Abdicated*	*Died*
51.	HEIZEI	774	806	809	824
52.	SAGA	786	809	823	842
53.	JUNNA	786	823	833	840
54.	NIMMYŌ	810	833		850
55.	MONTOKU	827	850		858
56.	SEIWA	850	858	876	880
57.	YŌZEI	868	876	884	949
58.	KŌKŌ	830	884		887
59.	UDA	867	887	897	931
60.	DAIGO	885	897	930	930
61.	SUZAKU	923	930	946	952
62.	MURAKAMI	926	946		967
63.	REIZEI	950	967	969	1011
64.	EN'YŪ	959	969	984	991
65.	KAZAN	968	984	986	1008
66.	ICHIJŌ	980	986	1011	1011
67.	SANJŌ	976	1011	1016	1017
68.	GO-ICHIJŌ	1008	1016	1036	1036
69.	GO-SUZAKU	1009	1036	1045	1045
70.	GO-REIZEI	1025	1045		1068
71.	GO-SANJŌ	1034	1068	1072	1073
72.	SHIRAKAWA	1053	1072	1086	1129
73.	HORIKAWA	1079	1086		1107
74.	TOBA	1103	1107	1123	1156
75.	SUTOKU	1119	1123	1141	1164
76.	KONOE	1139	1141		1155
77.	GO-SHIRAKAWA	1127	1155	1158	1192
78.	NIJŌ	1143	1158	1165	1165
79.	ROKUJŌ	1164	1165	1168	1176
80.	TAKAKURA	1161	1168	1180	1181
81.	ANTOKU	1178	1180	1183	1185
82.	GO-TOBA	1180	1183	1198	1239
83.	TSUCHIMIKADO	1195	1198	1210	1231

Posthumous name	*Born*	*Acceded*	*Abdicated*	*Died*
84. JUNTOKU	1197	1210	1221	1242
85. CHŪKYŌ	1218	1221	1221	1234
86. GO-HORIKAWA	1212	1221	1232	1234
87. SHIJŌ	1231	1232		1242
88. GO-SAGA	1220	1242	1246	1272
89. GO-FUKAKUSA	1243	1246	1259	1304
90. KAMEYAMA	1249	1259	1274	1305
91. GO-UDA	1267	1274	1287	1324
92. FUSHIMI	1265	1287	1298	1317
93. GO-FUSHIMI	1288	1298	1301	1336
94. GO-NIJŌ	1285	1301		1308
95. HANAZONO	1297	1308	1318	1348
96. GO-DAIGO	1288	1318		1339
97. GO-MURAKAMI	1328	1339		1368
98. CHŌKEI	1343	1368	1383	1394
99. GO-KAMEYAMA	1350	1383	1392	1424
100. GO-KOMATSU	1377	1392	1412	1433
101. SHŌKŌ	1401	1412		1428
102. GO-HANAZONO	1419	1428	1464	1470
103. GO-TSUCHIMIKADO	1442	1464		1500
104. GO-KASHIWABARA	1464	1500		1526
105. GO-NARA	1496	1526		1557
106. ŌGIMACHI	1517	1557	1586	1593
107. GO-YŌZEI	1571	1586	1611	1617
108. GO-MIZUNOO	1596	1611	1629	1680
109. MEISHŌ (ER)	1623	1629	1643	1696
110. GO-KŌMYŌ	1633	1643		1654
111. GOSAI	1637	1654	1663	1685
112. REIGEN	1654	1663	1687	1732
113. HIGASHIYAMA	1675	1687	1709	1709
114. NAKAMIKADO	1701	1709	1735	1737
115. SAKURAMACHI	1720	1735	1747	1750
116. MOMOZONO	1741	1747		1762

Posthumous name	*Born*	*Acceded*	*Abdicated*	*Died*
117. GO-SAKURAMACHI (ER)	1740	1762	1770	1813
118. GO-MOMOZONO	1758	1770		1779
119. KŌKAKU	1771	1779	1817	1840
120. NINKŌ	1800	1817		1846
121. KŌMEI	1831	1846		1867
122. MEIJI (Mutsuhito)	1852	1867		1912
123. TAISHŌ (Yoshihito)	1879	1912		1926
124. SHŌWA (Hirohito)	1901	1926		1989
125. The present emperor (Akihito)	1933	1989		

Glossary

Amaterasu	The sun goddess, legendary imperial ancestress
Arahitogami	A human being regarded as a living god
Bakufu	'Camp government': government under a shogun (q.v.)
Bushido	The code of honour of the samurai (q.v.) class
Daijosai	A protracted inaugural rite for a new emperor, involving mystical communion with Amaterasu
Daimyo	'Great names': feudal lords
Genro	Elder statesmen; those who had held high political office in the Meiji period
Go-Sekke	The five families descended from the Fujiwara
Han	The fief of a *daimyo*
Heika	'Majesty' as a title
Ho-o	A retired emperor in Buddhist priestly orders
Junshi	The suicide of a samurai on the death of his lord
Kami	A superior, supernatural entity
Kamikaze	'Divine Wind'
Kana	Two phonetic syllabaries for writing Japanese
Kashikodokoro	One of the imperial Shinto shrines, which contains a replica of the sacred mirror, one of the three items comprising the imperial regalia
Kenji	The other two items of the regalia: the sword and the jewel
Kigensetsu	National Foundation Day (11 February)
Kojiki	The earliest written chronicle of Japan
Kokutai	'The essence of the nation': the central ideological basis of Japanese patriotism from *c.* 1880 to 1945
Kotaishi	The crown prince of Japan (also *Togu*)
Kuge	The noble families whose members comprised the imperial court in Kyoto

Kunaisho	The Imperial Household Ministry established in the Meiji period (now Kunaicho, an administrative agency)
Kazoku	The nobility formed from the *kuge* and the *daimyo* in the Meiji period
Mikado	An obsolete word for the emperor
Misasagi	An imperial tomb
Naiku	The inner shrine at Ise
Niinami matsuri	An annual Shinto rite, when the emperor offers the first of the new rice at the palace shrines
Ryobu Shinto	The doctrine that Shinto gods are avatars of Buddha
Samurai	The feudal military class
Sanshu no Shinki	The imperial regalia
Seppuku	Ritual suicide (also known as *hara-kiri*)
Shikken	A regent in early medieval times
Shingon	An esoteric school of Japanese Buddhism
Sokui-rei	The essential first element of the accession rites
Tanka	A formal poem of thirty-one syllables
Tatami	Straw mats covered with finely woven grass and edged with fabric, formerly used as a dais of honour. Now traditional floor covering
Tenno	'Heavenly King': used to refer to the emperor
Togu	The crown prince (see also *Kotaishi*)
Torii	Symbolic gate at the approach to a Shinto shrine
Uji	A clan
Yata kagami	The sacred mirror
Zen	The meditative Buddhist sects

Further Reading

GENERAL

D.C. Holtom — *The National Faith of Japan,* London, Kegan Paul, 1938

R.H.P. Mason & J.G. Caiger — *A History of Japan,* Cassell Australia, 1972

R. Ponsonby-Fane — *The Imperial House of Japan,* Kyoto, Ponsonby Memorial Society, 1959

R. Ponsonby-Fane — *Sovereign and Subject,* Kyoto, Ponsonby Memorial Society, 1962

G.B. Sansom — *Japan: A Short Cultural History,* London, Cresset Library, 1987

MEDIEVAL

M.E. Berry — *The Culture of Civil War in Kyoto,* University of California, 1994

Robert Borgen — *Sugawara no Michizane and the Early Heian Court,* University of Hawaii, 1994

Ivan Morris — *The World of the Shining Prince,* Oxford, OUP, 1964

H. Paul Varley — *Imperial Restoration in Medieval Japan,* New York, Columbia University Press, 1971

EDO PERIOD

Herschel Webb — *The Japanese Imperial Institution in the Tokugawa Era,* New York, Columbia University Press, 1968

MEIJI

Carol Gluck — *Japan's Modern Myths,* Princeton, Princeton University Press, 1985

SHOWA

Thomas Crump	*The Death of an Emperor,* London, Constable, 1989
Stephen S. Large	*Emperor Hirohito and Showa Japan,* London, Routledge, 1992
Willard Price	*Japan and the Son of Heaven,* New York, Duell, Sloan & Pearce, 1945
David Titus	*Palace and Politics in Prewar Japan,* New York, Columbia University Press, 1974
Elizabeth Gray Vining	*Windows for the Crown Prince,* London, Michael Joseph, 1952

Index